AF471035

TWO HALVES OF A WHOLE

Torah Guidelines for Marriage

TWO HALVES OF A WHOLE

Torah Guidelines for Marriage

Book One:

From Woman to Woman: On Being a Wife

written by Tehilla Abramov and Bracha Goetz

based on Tehilla Abramov's lecture series on Shalom Bayis

Book Two:

From Man to Man: On Being a Husband

written by Rabbi Yirmiyohu Abramov and Shmuel Goldstein

based on Rabbi Abramov's lecture series on Shalom Bayis

TARGUM\FELDHEIM

Rabbi CHAIM P. SCHEINBERG

KIRYAT MATTERSDORF
PANIM MEIROT 2.
JERUSALEM, ISRAEL

הרב חיים פנחס שיינברג
ראש ישיבת "תורה אור"
ומורה הוראה דקרית מטרסדורף
ירושלים טל.נוי52

The sacred institution of marriage is seriously threatened in our times. Shocking statistics about divorce rates combine with countless reports about unhappy marriages and unstable families to paint a sad picture of what happens after the *mazel tov*s are said.

A major source of their problem is the lack of proper guidance which *chasan* and *kallah* receive in preparing themselves for a life together based on the foundation of halachah and Torah *hashkafah.* Rabbi Yirmiyohu and Rebbetzin Tehilla Abramov, under the guidelines of *Gedolei Torah,* have made a historic contribution to educating the public in the area of Jewish family life through the seminars and programs of Jewish Marriage Education International. Their experience has convinced them that there is a desperate need for the material taught in these seminars to be made available in book form.

The two sections of the marriage book, one for men and one for women, have been written with great sensitivity and in an engaging style. I offer the authors my *berachah* that this publication will enhance their efforts to dispel ignorance about the Torah approach to marriage and will bring *shalom bayis* to homes throughout *Klal Yisrael.*

Rabbi Chaim Pinchas Scheinberg
Iyar, 5754

הרב ישראל גנס

רח׳ פנים מאירות 2

קרית מטרסדורף, ירושלים 94 473

טלפון 531782

The subject of *shalom bayis* has, sadly enough, deteriorated greatly in this generation. There are many factors contributing to this — the lack of proper education in *emunah ubitachon,* the lack of working on one's character traits, and the lack of proper guidance and preparation for marital life according to Torah guidelines with the right balance of esteem and holiness.

Not enough people are involved in this holy work, so that whoever lends a shoulder to this task is contributing much in the field.

Rabbi Yirmiyohu Abramov, *shlita,* and his worthy Rebbetzin, Tehilla, *tichya,* have undertaken this sacred mission, and this book now being published after years of rich experience and arduous labor in the field is just one facet of their endeavors.

I only perused this work briefly, but I have full faith in the esteemed writer and his wife that what they produce can only be a superior product for which they should be heartily encouraged.

May Hashem richly reward those who do good with commensurate goodness.

With hearty blessings to those involved in this mitzvah.

Yisrael Ganz

Acknowledgments

Our thanks to:

— Mr. Shmuel Goldstein, whose creative writing skills have enabled this book to emerge.

— all those whose encouragement was the force which made this book a reality.

With heartful gratitude to
Hashem Yisborach

*Yirmiyohu Abramov
Adar, 5754*

— Mrs. Bracha Goetz, whose creative writing skills have enabled this book to emerge.

— my mother, Mrs. Rivka Katz, Mrs. M. L. Mashinsky, Mrs. Chava Dumas and Ruchama King for their assistance with the manuscript.

— all the wonderful wives whose authentic experiences appear in this book and who serve as an inspiration to us all. (For obvious reasons, names and places have all been changed.)

— all whose encouragement was the force which made this book a reality.

With heartfelt gratitude to
Hashem Yisborach

*Tehilla Abramov
Adar, 5754*

In memory of my dear parents,

לעלוי נשמת
אמי מורתי
מרת חסיה (הטי) ב"ר אברהם איסר
אברמוב ע"ה
נלב"ע ב׳ תשרי תשנ"ב
ת.נ.צ.ב.ה.

לעלוי נשמת
אבי מורי
ר׳ אוריאל חיים ב"ר ישראל
אברמוב ז"ל
נלב"ע ב׳ ניסן תשכ"ד
ת.נ.צ.ב.ה.

Yirmiyahu Abramov

In memory of my dear father,

לעלוי נשמת אבי מורי
ר׳ ישראל אלכסנדר ב"ר חיים בן ציון כץ ז"ל
נלבע טו אדר תשמ"ה
ת.נ.צ.ב.ה.

and להבדיל לחיים טובים וארוכים

in deep appreciation to my dear mother תחי״י
May she continue to be a source of growth and inspiration
ad meah v'esrim shanah, and may she have much *nachas* from her
children, grandchildren and great-grandchildren.

Tehilla Abramov

Dedicated to:

     The Ringo family of South Africa, whose charitable deeds and love and dedication in promoting Jewish education are a tribute to their illustrious forefathers from Dvinsk.

     May Hashem grant them the merit to continue in their noble unsung deeds.

Table of Contents

Book One:

From Woman to Woman:
On Being a Wife

ONE

Made in Heaven

They were both in intense pain at the prospect of going through with this. Still, the childless couple approached Rabbi Shimon bar Yochai and requested that he write them a bill of divorce. Although they enjoyed a happy marriage, each of them wanted children very much, and so they had finally decided to seek a divorce.

The great Sage looked upon them thoughtfully and replied, "I will be willing to fulfill your request, but may I suggest that you first prepare a feast marking this occasion? After all, you were united in marriage with a feast, so it would be a good idea for you two to terminate your bond in the same way."

The couple followed the Rabbi's unusual advice and invited family and friends to their parting banquet. In the midst of the meal, the husband stood up and declared out loud to his wife: "My dear wife, everyone understands the unfortunate circumstances which led to our upcoming divorce. I would like you to remember our relationship very favorably despite our imminent separation. Please, on leaving this home, immediately choose whichever thing in this house is most precious to you. In fact, it will be taken to your parents' home for you. No matter how valuable it may be — it will soon be your very own, most prized possession."

It didn't take long at all for the woman to decide exactly what she most wanted. And so, in order to insure that her desire would really be fulfilled, throughout the evening she discreetly but repeatedly refilled her husband's wine goblet. After the drink had taken effect, and he was soundly asleep, she ordered the servants to carry him to her parents' home.

When the man awoke and discovered what had taken place, he looked at his wife with a puzzled expression.

"I just followed your instructions," she answered. "You are the most prized possession I could possibly think of!"

They returned to Rabbi Shimon, and he prayed for them. Soon, they were blessed with children (*Shir HaShirim Rabbah* 1).

A wife's greatest treasure is her husband, even when his value is not so apparent to her. And, as this story illustrates, even when a marriage appears to be in its final stage of dissolution, it can be rebuilt by the efforts and intuition of a loving wife.

*   *   *

"And G-d created man in His image. In the image of G-d He created him, male and female He created them and He blessed them." *(Bereshis* 1:27*)*

This is a very deep and complex passage. But one concept we are able to understand from it is that man and woman *together* combine to form the G-dly image intended for human beings. Only after both man and woman were created did G-d bless them as one unit. It was not until then that the name Adam was given for mankind in general.

Our Sages explain that Adam was chosen as the human being's name because this creation was made from the *adamah*, earth. Animals, however, were also created from the earth, and they were given another name: *be-hamah* or *ba mah*, meaning, "It is what it is."

Given their shared origin, why was one name chosen for mankind and another for animals? The Maharal explains that the resolution to this question lies in the common potential shared by the two entities — human beings and earth. The earth possesses the power to make things grow. Similarly, human beings are the only creations made with the ability to grow by developing their own potentials. Every other creation is limited by the nature with which it was created, by its given nature. Only human beings have the ability to rise above their inborn tendencies and give them new direction.

Although blessed with this possibility, human beings must nevertheless labor in order to realize their growth potential. As mentioned above, the name Adam was given after the creation of both man and woman, implying that the union of man and woman in marriage is a primary catalyst for the development of each partner's individual potential to the utmost.

The essence of the growth process spurred by marriage involves stepping beyond one's individual identity. Before marriage, the bride and the groom are each concerned with their own aspirations and ambitions. Marriage alters this self-concern significantly and enables them to become more attentive to each other's needs. The two can begin growing beyond themselves to become fused into a single cohesive unit. As it states, "And he shall cling to his wife...and they shall become one flesh" (*Bereshis* 2:24).

*   *   *

Dina was staring at herself in the mirror. She looked miserable, and she knew it was all *his* fault. He never cared about how she looked. Never noticing her clothes, her face, nothing. Nothing except the washed dishes that he found *still* greasy! Why even bother trying? When was the last time he had given her a compliment? She couldn't even remember back that far. Probably not since before they were married. But then he had treated her so completely differently.

"This marriage was a terrible mistake," Dina thought to herself for the sixth time that afternoon. "I would have been so much happier married to Aaron. He's much more my type. I can't believe this is happening. Now what in the world am I going to do?"

*   *   *

We live in a throwaway society. It's a mentality that affects every aspect of our lives, not just the ecological equilibrium. As easily as we dispose of plastic and paper, cars and appliances that weren't meant to last forever, so do we easily throw aside relationships at the first sign of trouble. Faced with evidence of incompatibility, both halves of a couple are quick to wonder whether they chose the "wrong item" and if they should exchange it for another, more suitable one.

Demographers project that half of all first marriages made today will end in divorce. Six out of ten second marriages will probably collapse. But when most couples marry, they feel that *their* marriage will not succumb to this trend of our times. Theirs, they hope, will last. Hoping is not enough, though. Like a profession, marriage requires preparation and constant "refreshers" to stay on top of it. Nothing could be a more helpful gift to a newlywed couple than a wealth of practical information about the positive attitudes and realistic expectations that make marriages work well.

Helping a marriage not merely to survive, but also to thrive, is a goal extensively supported by our rich Torah wisdom. Within Judaism, marriage is considered the ideal state in which human beings may develop their full potential. And marriages, we learn, are made in heaven. This may be a very difficult concept for some to genuinely believe.

*   *   *

A Roman matron once asked Rabbi Yossi ben Chalafta, "What does G-d do every day since He created the world?"

Reb Yossi answered, "He is making matches — bringing couples together so that they can get married."

The Roman matron scoffed, "Why, that's not difficult to do at all! I have one thousand male and one thousand female servants. I could easily match them all off in one night!"

Reb Yossi said to her, "Maybe you think it is as easy as that, but we have learned that G-d considers it more difficult than parting the Red Sea."

After that, the matron simply couldn't resist trying her own hand at matchmaking. She paired off all her one thousand male and one thousand female servants that very evening.

Well, the morning after was not such a splendid one.

Her couples surrounded her, complaining, insulted and even injured. Some had broken legs, some had broken arms and some had swollen, black eyes. They clearly did not want the spouses the matron had picked out for them.

Totally exasperated, the matron sent for Reb Yossi and asked him, "How on earth does G-d do this?"

Reb Yossi replied very simply, "G-d uses His infinite wisdom to make matches, deciding who will be best for whom. And He brings them together from different parts of the world in order to match them up perfectly. This He has done since He first created the Universe."

The Roman matron then admitted, "There is no G-d like your G-d" (*Bereshis Rabbah* 68:4).

*   *   *

In the Talmud it is written (*Sotah* 2a), "Forty days before conception it is decreed in heaven: 'The daughter of this person is for the son of that person!' " In the making of matches we do not buy into the popularly accepted element of luck, or coincidence. We do not believe that meeting our destined partners comes about through the tossing of dice, that our fates hang on the thread of a "chance" meeting. On the contrary, it has all been extremely well thought-out and very carefully planned in advance.

*   *   *

Reuven Schwartz was a successful diamond dealer in his mid-thirties. He enjoyed traveling, meeting people, making connections. When he wasn't on the road, he lived in the midst of a thriving Jewish community in New York. His sister and her family lived close by, and numerous other relatives lived within the city. But despite his own and their efforts to find him a suitable mate, he was still a bachelor.

He was on a Tuesday night flight, anxiously anticipating his return to New York in time for the Jewish New Year that Wednesday night. He had just spent four productive days in Bangkok, the tail end of a month-long business trip in the Far East. Flight 081 would arrive in New York the following morning, just in time for *erev Rosh HaShanah.*

Exhausted from his heavy schedule, Reuven boarded the plane, settled into his seat and relaxed while his fellow passengers continued to organize themselves for takeoff. He did not notice the worried-looking official approaching his seat.

"Excuse me, are you Mr. Schwartz?"

Reuven opened his eyes. "Hmm? Yes?"

A short, stout man in a flight uniform stood in the aisle looking right at him. "I'm sorry, sir, but our computer has just spotted a discrepancy. Your ticket is invalid. You will have to come with me."

Reuven's drowsiness vanished. "What? That's impossible! I've been using that ticket all month!"

"I'm sorry, sir, but the last stub for this flight is missing. I'm sure it is just an oversight, but we have to follow regulations."

Reuven was aghast. "But I'll buy a new ticket! This is the last flight to New York and I have to be on it!"

Nearby passengers sympathetically looked on. One man leaned over and offered to help. The clerk just shook his head. "Please, sir. There is no time to write up a new ticket. The plane is almost done refueling. You must get off this plane and come with me to our office!"

Traveling on a tight schedule close to a Jewish holiday had always worried Reuven, but in fifteen years, nothing like this had ever happened to him.

"What's going on?" he thought. "There's nothing wrong with my ticket. This is impossible! I can't stay in Bangkok for Rosh HaShanah!"

The clerk refused to budge without Reuven, but at the office there was no way to straighten things out in time...and his flight left without him. A call to New York just a few minutes later confirmed that the oversight had been a simple numerical error. His travel agent had made a small mistake, causing Reuven to be stranded in Bangkok on *erev Rosh HaShanah.*

Still in the airline's office, Reuven thought rapidly. From a conversation he'd had earlier that week, he knew that scarcely any of the observant Jews in Bangkok remained there for the High Holy Days. Most arranged to be in Europe at that time, so he did not have many options available.

"Are there any flights to Hong Kong?" he asked. Fortunately, there was one scheduled for the morning. Hong Kong was the nearest city with a Jewish community that he could join for Rosh HaShanah.

Reuven finally arrived in Hong Kong, completely drained. He made several inquiring phone calls from the airport and was very happy when a Mrs. Fisher invited him to spend the holiday with her family.

"What a relief not to have to stay in a hotel again," thought Reuven when the taxi dropped him off at the Fisher home. Reuven could not help but wonder at the strange turn of events that had him celebrating Rosh HaShanah in Hong Kong.

After three days as a guest with the Fisher family, Reuven had a clearer understanding of why events had worked in this mysterious way. Joining the warm family for all the *yom tov* meals, Reuven had become acquainted with the Fishers' eldest daughter, Sara.

Reuven did not leave Hong Kong in a hurry. Instead, he checked into a nearby hotel after Rosh HaShanah. He and Sara needed more time to get to know each other.

Twenty-five years later, Reuven still jokes with Sara about the travel agent who made a "mistake" with his ticket. "To our great good fortune!" he says with a wink at his wife.

* * *

Is this story an exceptional one? Well, for Reuven and Sara it surely is. But if we've ever listened to other married couples excitedly telling the story of how they got together, the same sense of awe about the way things amazingly fell into place is nearly always palpable. Events are set in train (or on planes!) years before the couple may ever come together.

One famous example where the series of events leading up to a union was more evident than usual, involved a great Torah scholar, the Rashash, Rav Shmuel Shtershun, who also ran a free-loan fund for the poor.

* * *

One day, a tailor named Reb Zalman came to borrow money. The Rashash granted him a loan of three hundred rubles, to be paid back in one year, and recorded the transaction in his ledger.

One year later, as agreed, Reb Zalman came to the home of the Rashash to return the money. Seeing that the great Rabbi was deeply immersed in Torah study, he did not want to disturb him. He quietly came into the room, excused himself for interrupting, put the three hundred rubles on the Rabbi's desk and left.

Rav Shmuel tucked the money into the volume he was studying and continued to learn. By the time he finished, he had completely forgotten about the money and returned the Torah volume he had been studying, with the money inside, to its shelf.

A few weeks later, Rav Shmuel reviewed his ledger and noticed that the loan to Reb Zalman was still outstanding. He sent for Reb Zalman to inquire about the money.

Of course, Reb Zalman claimed that he had returned the loan on the very day it was due. But there were no witnesses, and Rav Shmuel had no recollection of the matter.

They agreed to go to the rabbinical court for a decision. Since it was ruled that it was the word of one man against another, Reb Zalman would have to swear that he repaid the loan, and he would then be absolved of his debt. The Rashash, however, was concerned that he might be causing a fellow Jew to swear falsely, so he dropped the charge. The case was closed.

Meanwhile, though, the news had spread that the simple tailor had the audacity to challenge the word of the saintly scholar, Rav Shmuel! People stopped doing business with the tailor. Mocked and degraded, he eventually had to take his family and leave the town a broken man.

A year passed, and the Rashash was once again studying from the same volume. Imagine his surprise when he opened it and noticed a large sum of money inside. It took just a moment for him to realize that this was the very money the tailor claimed he had returned!

Immediately, the Rashash sought out Reb Zalman. He found the tailor living in sad conditions in a desolate area. The Rashash begged Reb Zalman for forgiveness. He offered to run to every synagogue to announce that he had made a terrible mistake, and that the tailor was fully deserving of respect.

Reb Zalman, though, said that it was too late. People would not believe he was innocent. They would just say that the Rashash was doing it out of pity because he was a righteous person.

The Rashash knew Reb Zalman was right. A great injustice had been done. Now he would have to think of some way to rectify the situation. Rav Shmuel thought deeply for a few moments, and then he finally spoke. "If we make a match between my daughter and your son," the Rashash smiled, "we will be family, and no one will doubt your honesty and respectability."

Reb Zalman consented, and they arranged for their children to meet. The tailor's son and the Rashash's daughter were agreeable and so their wedding took place…

It was decreed in heaven that those two would marry, but (just as in our own marriages) a long series of events had to occur before this very unlikely match of the son of a simple tailor and the daughter of a renowned Sage could be arranged.

(Based on "The Forgotten Loan" in The Maggid Speaks)

*   *   *

Why is the concept of "marriages being made in heaven" so important? As incredible as it may seem, it is the basis for harmony in the home.

In the spiritual sense, the marital unit is a pre-existing entity. Both husband and wife are part of one whole which G-d intended to unite through marriage. The *Zohar* describes a marriage as the union of two half-souls. These halves were clothed in separate bodies as the soul descended upon the earth, only to be reunited by marriage. This soul bond is divinely predestined.

It is a long and absorbing journey, though, between the meeting and the true reuniting of two half-souls. Many make the error of assuming that if only they can succeed in finding their soulmates from amid the sea of souls, the rest is easy. The couple will live "happily ever after" because their marriage was "made in heaven." Actually, finding each other is a lifelong process. It involves challenging struggles which help each find out what the other half of his or her soul is all about, as well as a better understanding of what his or her own half contains.

Standing under the wedding canopy, a man and a woman begin their new life of growth together. Neither man nor woman is worth more than the other, for they are like the right and left hand of the same body, beginning to unite so that they can function as complementary parts of a complete whole. Becoming one is the purpose of marriage.

We believe that G-d is involved in the predestination of each unique pair, but free will remains an important factor. The decisions to develop or not to develop the potential inherent in the G-d-given match lie with each person. So when a man and woman marry, the two half-souls recognize each other perfectly well. The trouble lies with the two physical beings which are clothed in different garments. Each physical being brings with it its own set of different needs and peculiarities. The marriage was ordained in heaven, but must be carried out on earth with all its seemingly mundane challenges.

In the spiritual world, our souls may come from the same origin, but here on earth, we must deal with the realities of our earthly lives, which usually have very dissimilar origins. Coming from different homes and environments, and possessing different personalities, capabilities, experiences, strengths and weaknesses, we find that most of our characteristics do not fall into neat compartments of compatibility. These are just the raw materials with which each couple must work. The goal becomes to take these materials and to labor creatively to mold them into the harmonious ideal that is the very essence of what was foreseen when our marriage was made in heaven.

We need to understand that in marriages made in heaven there will always be difficulties. Growth pangs can bring the two halves ever closer. Problems that bring pain must not be ignored. The Torah approach is to confront the issues, and clarify the source of pain and find out how best to treat it.

Although it stresses the sanctity of marriage, Judaism has always allowed for the possibility of divorce. This is a very sad occurrence, described by our Sages as a time when the "altar sheds tears." The big problem today, though, is that we see couples considering divorce when they have never been given a true realization of what marriage is. The Torah approach is to confront the problematic issues, seek the guidance of rabbis and qualified, Torah-guided counselors, and opt for divorce only when all that remains of the bond between the couple are the halachic formalities.

During a flush of disappointment, when feeling that our choice in husbands was mistaken, if we can grasp hold of the idea that our chosen partner was destined for us, then we will be more motivated to make the marriage work as it was designed — with the potential to work. Problems in marriage are signals, not to divorce, but to identify the problem more clearly and get to work on its resolution. Divorce should be only an absolutely last resort — after exhausting all avenues of reconciliation.

Under the wedding canopy we receive a blessing. It is that our marriages should be filled with the kind of ecstatic joy experienced by the first married couple, Adam and Chava, in the Garden of Eden.

What was the nature of their bliss? When two people marry and conflicts inevitably arise, it's common for doubts to cross their minds. "Perhaps if I had married so-and-so it would have been different" pops into their heads too often. Then, instead of working out the differences, they channel more energy into feeling gypped and angry at having made a serious mistake.

Adam and Chava never wasted any time or energy wondering if they were right for each other. They were the only two people on earth, so it was absolutely clear to each of them that they were the appropriate spouses for one another. No doubts were ever entertained, and so all energies could be focused on making the marriage even better. Their commitment to each other was clearly an eternal one.

Each marriage, in our times, replicates the original marriage of Adam and Chava. If the name of our spouse was called out in heaven forty days before our conception, surely our marriage has G-d's seal of approval as much as the marriage of Adam and Chava does. Who didn't experience the sense of G-d's guiding hand leading us to each other? And yet we doubt, we waver internally, we compare our relationship to our friends' relationships, not realizing there is only the two of us — no one else.

An absolute belief that we were meant to be married to our spouse leads us to the awareness that G-d is between us; that G-d has been guiding us, and will continue to guide us through the ups and downs and twists and turns of becoming one in our marriage. When will we be able to achieve the same joy as Adam and Chava? When the commitment to our spouse is absolute and unwavering.

The lesson of Adam and Chava is step one. To the degree that we accept our spouses as the ones intended for us by G-d, we will be able to save our energies for the more complicated and subtle art of making our marriages truly happy and vital ones.

TWO

Coming Down to Earth

In Europe, two great Chassidic rabbis once decided to make a match between their children and arranged for them to meet. The girl's father told his daughter all about the proposed groom, omitting one detail.

The moment the prospective bride-to-be saw the prospective groom, she burst into tears. Maybe he was all her father had claimed — kind, brilliant and pious — but he was also obviously lame. Without even speaking to him, the girl refused to consider the proposal.

The young man, however, insisted on speaking with her. Gently, he told her, "Forty days before I was conceived, a heavenly voice announced whom I would marry. I saw a vision of my bride. She would be a wonderful, kind person, with only one defect — she would be lame. I was filled with such sorrow when I saw the life of suffering she would endure that I prayed and cried and fasted so that G-d would remove the burden from her and instead give *me* the defect."

Then, looking intently at his prospective bride, he

whispered, "Thank G-d, my prayers were answered."

With new insight, the girl consented to the marriage, and her wedding was arranged with great joy.

(Adapted from Souled by Hanoch Teller)

*   *   *

This is not the kind of story that most of us could tell about our courtship experience. We are probably not on such a lofty spiritual plane to remember the visions that we had when we were only souls, not yet clothed in bodies. What we can most definitely relate to, however, is the shock that we find ourselves experiencing each time we recognize another one of the vast differences between ourselves and our husbands.

*   *   *

Five months after her wedding, Esther was in tears. She was sure she had made a grave mistake in marrying her husband. By nature, she was a very neat and tidy person. She liked everything to be in its proper place. Her husband, however, left his clothes strewn all over — his socks on the floor, his coat on the couch, his hat on the dish rack. Initially she was surprised, then dismayed, then agitated. As the days went by, she was often angry. She could no longer stand her husband's untidiness. And after he traipsed across the newly washed floor, without even thinking of taking off his muddy shoes, she was convinced that she had married the wrong man.

She consulted the counselor with whom she had studied about Jewish marriage before her wedding. After telling her all her woes, she was taken aback by the counselor's reaction.

"Terrific!" exclaimed Mrs. Kaye.

"What on earth is terrific about this?" Esther asked, bewildered.

"Well, don't you see? Now you have found out one of your differences. So with this recognition in mind, you are one step closer to working out a plan of action for how to handle this very real difference."

*　　*　　*

While marriages are made in heaven, married life is very much a down-to-earth experience.

*　　*　　*

A month after the wedding...

The alarm goes off. He rolls over and doesn't get up on time.

Her idea of "making dinner" is ordering in from a fast-food restaurant.

His personal hygiene needs radical improvement.

She can't detach her ear from the phone.

He yawns and turns to read the paper when she finally opens her heart to him.

Her moodiness and critical remarks are driving him crazy.

They are both horrified.

*　　*　　*

Do the conflicts and tension catch us by surprise? Of course they do. Our marriages do not measure up to the idealized visions we had of "merging" with our other halves, and we're disappointed. It's a far cry from the romantic images we dreamed of as brides-to-be. We had managed to get by just fine in life before, though we may have left our stockings strewn on the floor, and we may have had a tendency to interrupt people when we became excited, habits we were sure he would consider charming, or at least have the decency to overlook. But he *isn't* overlooking. He's getting impatient and annoyed. And so are we — as we discover more and more of the peculiar aspects of *his* character.

"It's a mistake!" we quickly fear. But what we need to keep remembering is: "G-d made this match. He put the two of us together. And *He* doesn't make mistakes." It's a cosmic thought that can produce cosmic changes.

A couple, after all, *is* made up of two different people — not two identical twins. "He is the one," we need to tell ourselves. "The challenge was designed, tailored and then personally handed to me by G-d."

Marriage involves recognizing our many down-to-earth differences — getting clarity about the distinctions between us. Because, as we know, we can't try to fit two puzzle pieces together well, if we don't see clearly what each puzzle piece really looks like.

Let's try replacing our habitual doubts with accurate, affirmative statements as quickly as we possibly can. If every time we missed a bus we debated whether or not we were living in the right neighborhood, working in the right profession, and whether or not there was a compassionate G-d, our energy would get sapped pretty fast, unnecessarily.

The next time we're feeling great, and we're all set to make our marriages work, and then our husbands go and spoil the whole atmosphere by complaining about our greasy plates *again*, let's take a good deep breath and consider. Courtship is a process in which two people construct masks to attract the other. When the masks come off, the marriage starts. Right now the masks are falling off with amazing rapidity. But instead of throwing up our arms in despair, let's clap our hands in celebration. Now our real life's work can begin!

Each spouse acts as a mirror to the other. Within marriage we possess a safe and also a holy framework to see ourselves honestly and do the fixing that we may have been putting off for years. The incompatibilities we experience between the two of us are not a sign that the marriage was a complete error. Rather, they indicate what married life is for — the long, hard work required to produce a masterpiece. That's the reason we two were put together.

Our husbands may be lame, or they may be vain. They may be short-tempered, or maybe just plain short. They may be too quiet or too loud, too stingy or too spendthrift, or possessed of any of a host of other physical or spiritual ailments. Nevertheless, as hard as it may seem to believe right at this moment, they are the ones destined to bring out our best.

We women, too (believe it or not), have our own shortcomings — many of which we may not even be aware of. But we still bring them along with us into a marriage. Sometimes, however, what an irate marriage partner perceives as a flaw in the other is actually no more than a different attitude.

As we said earlier, the fact is that the two halves of one couple come from different homes and environments. They have different personalities, capabilities, experiences, strengths and weaknesses. These may be the cause of many difficulties.

*   *   *

Judith and David were recently married. As they prepared to spend their first Shabbos alone together, they realized they did not have a special Shabbos tablecloth.

Looking very much like newlyweds, they lovingly started out on their shopping trip. Together, they strolled into a small home supplies store. As Judith inspected the selection, she knew exactly what would be perfect — a magnificent embroidered linen cloth just like the one her mother always used for Shabbos.

Meanwhile, David made his own choice — a simple, white, plastic one that would be practical and easy to clean.

When Judith saw what David had selected, she was shocked. When he saw her choice, he was appalled.

"But it's for Shabbos," she wailed. "We can't use plastic!"

He looked at the fine linen tablecloth and retorted, "But that would get ruined with just one wine spill!"

They began to argue. Suddenly her parents, too, were brought into the dispute. David said her family's decor had always been a little too showy for his tastes. Judith bristled. She told him maybe he didn't know the difference between showy and tasteful, and why should he, coming from the family that he did. They began to leave the store — she in tears, he in shock.

Just then the owner of the store rushed up to David and Judith. "I have the perfect match!" he said. They looked at him. In one of his hands was a thin, transparent plastic sheet to cover the fine linen tablecloth that was in his other hand.

They purchased the two items that went so well together — and got the message too. Their differences could work well together also. Yes, despite their differences — *no*, somehow even *because* of these differences — they, too, were a perfect match.

*   *   *

To the objective outsider, a sensible solution to a couple's dispute may seem so easily achievable. When under the strong influence of different backgrounds and tastes, however, personalities can clash profoundly over the most trivial things.

*   *   *

Rivky served "family style," putting big bowls of food on the table, so that everyone in the family could take his or her own portion. This is what her mother had always done. Danny harbored some hurt feelings at each meal that his wife didn't really care that much about him. *His* mother had always put the food directly on her son's plate. It took about eight years before Danny got enough clarity about what was causing his hurt feelings to express them to Rivky. After that, Rivky made an extra effort to remember to put Danny's food right onto his plate. This minor change didn't feel minor at all to Danny. He felt wonderful — and so did Rivky.

*   *   *

Even differences that seem trivial may in truth be laden with very heavy significance from our distinct up-bringings. During the course of their marriage, a husband and wife are in for all kinds of "surprises," discovering traits, habits and attitudes not expected in their new partnership. Convincing oneself that a serious mistake has been made weakens the ability to rise to the occasion, to resolve the conflict, to reach a compromise and to foster communication.

When our Sages taught us that "the same way that their faces differ, so do their personalities differ," they were certainly including spouses in that dictum. In addition to the individual distinctions resulting from being different people with different personalities from different backgrounds, we are also different from our husbands because of the very fundamental, innate difference that G-d put between us — that we are female and our other halves are male.

In Hebrew, the word for face is *panim* and the word for inside is *penim*. What is G-d communicating to us through the similarity of these two words? Just as our physical appearances differ, so do our inner make-ups differ. Some of the differences between us and our husbands result solely from the fact that they have male inner make-ups and we have female ones. This awareness can help prevent us from jumping so often to the incorrect conclusion that our many differences are signs that our marriages are mistakes. Instead, we can begin to recognize the seeming incompatibilities as signs of the challenge ahead of us: the challenge of working hard to discover how the two very different puzzle pieces can best fit together.

So, now that we know that we need to *expect* to find many differences and seeming incompatibilities, we can even try to be on the lookout for them. How boring it would be to be married to our clone in male form — and how stagnating. The effortless romances depicted in the media are fantasies. They confuse us. They make our expectations unrealistic. They are not real life.

Each and every predestined relationship carries within it the seeds of its own fruition. The potential is there, but the flowering of a marriage can come about only through a great deal of careful tending.

*   *   *

A great artist worked long and hard to paint a magnificent landscape, full of brilliant colors. His painting was covered up almost entirely, when somebody walked past, seeing just a very small piece of it — that happened to be black. "This one doesn't look too great to me," remarked the man. "You could do better!" The artist tried covering up his whole painting again, but a little white section was still exposed when somebody else hurried past. "Looks kind of boring to me," was the comment that this one tossed out.

*   *   *

The painting, of course, wasn't just black or just white. Both passersby were not seeing the whole picture. It is easy to be quick to judge the whole on the basis of a small part. What is much more difficult, but also that much more rewarding, is making the time and effort to see all the different colors in their unique and magnificent arrangements.

Some parts of marriage are black, some are white, and others may be pink or gray. Some times are happy, some times sad, some parts difficult; some parts flow more easily. But when drawn together with great thought and effort, they can be made into a true masterpiece.

"And G-d said: Let us make man in our image after our likeness, and let them have dominion over the fish of the sea and over the fowl of the air, and over the cattle and over all the earth..." (*Bereshis* 1:26).

In Hebrew, the word that means "let them have dominion" is "*v'eyirdu*." Rashi explains that this word comes from the same root and is very similar to the Hebrew word "*yeridah*," which means "going down." It was written as a warning to us in every aspect of our lives, including, of course, our very sacred marriages. It is warning us that if we do not use our potentials to struggle upward and try to override all the pressures pushing down on us, we will undoubtedly sink. There is no such thing as standing still. Either we are struggling mightily up a down escalator in life, or we are giving up and letting all the trials and tribulations that face us — as well as the crazy attitudes that are so prevalent around us — bring us, and our marriages, down.

If we find ourselves married to false expectations, now is the time to exchange them for the challenging ones found in our real lives. Marriage *can* be a bed of roses — but then that means we can expect to find lots of thorns along the way, too.

Marriages don't become marvelous automatically. The words, "And they lived happily ever after," have misled us more than we'd like to admit. The following ending may not be as tantalizing, but it is also less elusive — for it can genuinely be achieved: "And they lived happily ever after...a lot of hard work and effort!"

THREE

The Challenge of Acceptance

Korach's wife poisoned her husband's heart with jealousy. Then Korach, Moshe Rabbeinu's first cousin, began to set in motion a rebellion against Moshe because he himself wanted to be leader of the Jewish people.

Korach invited the men from the tribe of Reuven to join him. One of them, Onn, was impressed with Korach's arguments and decided to go along with him. When Onn returned home, he told his wife that he had joined Korach in the fight against Moshe.

Onn's wife, however, knew that Korach was motivated by evil desires. She tried hard to persuade her husband that he had nothing to gain by joining Korach's rebellion. But she was afraid that it was too late, as Onn had already sworn to Korach that he would help him.

So, in order to save her husband from disaster, Onn's wife then mixed some strong wine into his drink. He fell asleep immediately and slept heavily. Then she and her daughter went to sit at the entrance to their tent, where they could be seen publicly, without their hair coverings. This was something no other Jewish woman had ever done before.

Korach's messengers would not speak with or even look at Jewish women not dressed correctly, so when they arrived to tell Onn to come to Korach's secret gathering, they quickly turned around and left.

Several times Korach sent new messengers. But they, too, would not come close. Due to the wisdom of his wife, Onn escaped the destruction that was the lot of Korach and his family — when the earth suddenly opened up and swallowed them.

(Bemidbar Rabbah 18:15)

Our Sages teach us that the verse "The wise woman builds her home..." (*Mishlei* 14:1) refers to the wife of Onn, who used her wisdom to save her husband and her home from destruction. "But the foolish woman demolishes it with her own hands" (ibid.), refers to the wife of Korach, who brought ruination on her husband and her household

Now we can better understand the significance of the Hebrew term often used in describing women: *"akeres habayis."* As always, with Hebrew words, the term is packed with meaning. *"Habayis"* means the home, and *"akeres"* is derived from the word *"ikar,"* which means root, or essence, indicating that she is the most important part of the home. But *akeres* is similar to the word *"okeres,"* which means "uproot." The wife, through her actions, can choose to be the root of the home *or* its uprooter.

*   *   *

The Talmud teaches us that "Everything comes from the woman." An example is told of a righteous man who married a wicked woman, and he became *"wicked like her,"* whereas a righteous woman married a wicked man, and he became *"righteous like her."*

The completion of the state of goodness in creation was not man; it was woman. As the Talmud elaborates, only through his wife does a man become a true man: "How good are your tents, Yaakov, your small sanctuaries, Yisrael" (*Bemidbar* 24:5). How can these words be explained? 'Good' refers to the woman. It is she who is capable of uplifting Yaakov to become Yisrael, his loftier, full potential. It is she who is capable of raising her tent to become a small sanctuary.

A home is a mirror of the wife. The prevailing atmosphere is created by her. Therefore, even though it is ideal for both partners to make a joint effort and accept equal responsibility for improving their relationship, it sometimes happens that only one partner rises to the challenge.

If it is the woman, she *can* still progress in improving the relationship. She can still accomplish this without her husband's efforts, through the use of her special, G-d-given tools and powers. We know that women were created with an extra dimension of wisdom (*Bereshis Rabbah* 18:1). If the husband is reluctant to make changes, or to admit to a faulty relationship, or to seek help for their problems, the wife still can achieve tremendous results.

A person can improve another person's behavior indirectly by improving his own behavior. We can bring about amazing changes in our homes (which may include uncooperative husbands) by changing ourselves and having our husbands, ever so slowly, but ultimately, learn from our example.

This idea, then, gives light to the beautiful explanation of the verse: "*Vehu yimshol bach* — And he will rule over you" (*Bereshis* 3:16). The words *"yimshol bach"* usually mean "to rule over you." Since *"vehu"* means "and he," the phrase could be translated, "And he shall rule over you," referring to a husband ruling over his wife. But those same words have another meaning as well: "to learn from your example." Therefore, *"Vehu yimshol bach"* can also be translated: "He will learn from your example."

What we need to continually refocus on is what *we* are obligated to do, not what the other is obligated to do. We should try very hard not to pay attention to our husbands' obligations to us, but rather to our own obligations as wives.

*   *   *

There is a famous story of two water carriers who lived in Radin. Both of them used to do the same work every day, dragging the huge, empty buckets to the well outside the village, filling them with water and pulling on the rope to raise the full containers. Then they carried them on their shoulders back to the village and went from door to door, giving them out. The two were old, but they did this heavy work day in, day out.

When one of them was asked what kind of life he had, he smiled and said, "Oh, it's a *beautiful* life! I sure am thankful G-d gives me the strength to do what I have to do each day. I really enjoy giving out water to the people in this village. Imagine if I didn't bring them water! What sort of a life would they have?"

When the other water carrier, who did exactly the same job, was asked how *his* life was, he sighed, "Just *awful!* What do you think? Can't you see how hard I have to work? I haven't got the strength to carry all these buckets, that seem to weigh a ton, every single day! And I don't see why the people can't go and get their own water! Why does an old man like me have to do all this work?"

*   *   *

The quality of a person's life is determined by the attitude the individual chooses to hold about his life. Some will say, "Well, I don't have a positive attitude toward life because I wasn't born with that kind of disposition." It's true that some people may have to work harder than others to attain a positive attitude, but it is still attainable if enough *intellectual* energy is directed toward that aim. That's what so many of us don't realize. Happiness is the result of a cognitive process. It involves developing the mental flexibility and creativity to see things from different, and essentially more enlightened, perspectives. The more we exercise these intellectual abilities, the easier it will be to enjoy life.

Changing diapers, scrubbing floors, washing dishes — these can easily be considered "dirty work." But with just a little mental exertion added on to the physical exertion, the underlying joyful purpose of these chores can become clear, and the work actually uplifting.

The Talmud relates a story about Rabbi Akiva, who once went on a journey. He took with him a donkey to carry his luggage, a rooster to wake him in the morning and a candle by which to learn Torah.

He arrived at a certain village at the end of the day looking for a place to sleep for the night. But not one of the villagers would allow him to sleep at his home. Having no other option, he camped in a nearby field for the night.

It was not long before a lion came and devoured his

donkey, a cat ate his rooster and the wind blew out his candle.

Akiva got to see how all these troubles had really been for his good the next morning, when he visited the village again and saw that robbers had attacked the villagers and taken them as prisoners. In fact, the robbers had passed through the field where he had been sleeping, but there was no donkey's braying to give him away; neither was there a rooster crowing nor light for them to find him.

All G-d does is for the best.

A positive attitude, sprinkled with a sense of humor, can greatly assist in bridging troubled waters. A deep understanding that *gam zu letovah* — yes, even *this* problem is actually for the best — can immensely ease the strain of a struggle. Hardships and troubles, whether concerning finances, children or illness, can be overcome and sometimes even transformed into blessings when a positive view is reached.

A couple that tries hard to confront the many challenges of marriage from a positive perspective will discover that their experiences can actually present an opportunity for mutual growth and understanding. People who go through such challenges and difficulties together usually become closer to each other.

*   *   *

Rabbi Yosef Chaim Zonnenfeld was a leading figure in the old *yishuv* in Jerusalem. His advice and assistance were prized by all. His admirers supported him financially, and Rabbi Yosef Chaim, in turn, distributed much of these donations to the needy.

One year, as *erev Pesach* crept closer, the expected

donations had still not materialized. When the money finally did come, the Rabbi's good wife realized that it was too late to both distribute the charity among the members of the community and do her own preparations and shopping for the holiday. She consulted her husband, who instructed her to distribute the money.

"Some people," he explained, "need to have the *yom tov* necessities in order to celebrate a joyful holiday. As for us, our joy comes from within. We will have a happy holiday regardless."

If we can concentrate on the joy that we can give to our other halves, our anxiety and disappointment over problems arising from external factors will not be able to disturb our marital relationships. It isn't easy — but it *is* within our reach.

*   *   *

From her first appearance at the beginning of *Bereshis*, we see that woman was imbued with two seemingly contradictory traits. While the Torah refers to the first man by only one name, Adam, it calls the first woman both Chava and "*ishah.*" The name Chava was given to emphasize how she was "the mother of all life" (*Bereshis* 3:20). Her paramount function was to give life, to nurture and to make the home. Yet woman was also called *ishah,* the root of the word indicating woman's ability to develop her *ishiyus,* her own unique personality and talents, aside from the demands made on her in her universal role as mother.

The ability to fuse together "motherhood" and "personality" result from the *binah yeseirah,* the extra dimension of understanding with which we can comprehend differences between people and know how best to deal with them. This additional measure of insight which G-d bestows upon every woman was given to her primarily so that she would be able to fulfill her role as wife and mother and yet maintain a sense of self. What then is the ideal fusion of these two traits?

"*Kol kevudah bas melech penimah* — The glory of a princess is inward" (*Tehillim* 45:14). Beyond referring to the womanly virtue of modesty, this verse is meant to demonstrate a fundamental Torah ideal. For in Torah Judaism, the woman is not a seeker of the public eye. Her fine qualities and talents are directed inward, to home and family. In contrast, the man is the one whose role is directed outward — to act in society at large.

But rather than viewing the woman's position as demeaning, the Torah exalts the role of mother and homemaker. The home is everything in Judaism. So she who nurtures and runs the home is really in a position of the utmost importance and responsibility. A woman's ability to internalize this truth and recognize the importance of what she does results in the highest form of personality development.

When the Jewish woman recognizes the significance of all her actions within her home, she is able to perceive how the Jewish home can be considered a mini-Temple. Washing dishes, scrubbing floors or mending clothes all acquire a new dimension. When the Jewish woman knows she is coordinating a service of G-d within the realm of her own home, like the High Priest in the Beis HaMikdash (Temple), her joy is radiant, and the nature of her home is transformed. It becomes a great deal more than a physical building.

Every man views his home as a sanctuary allowing him to relax from the constant pressure society places on him. Daily, he must confront criticism, fulfill the demanding expectations made of him, and keep pace with the competition. His home — with its essence being his wife — should be, by contrast, a place of welcome and acceptance.

*   *   *

By the time they were married, Ilana was certain that she knew everything there was to know about her husband Jonathan, so she was pleasantly surprised as their first year of marriage unfolded to discover new areas of creativity and ingenuity in him. Not all her discoveries were of such a pleasant nature, though.

Jonathan, it turned out, was an ardent rock collector. His collection was rare and impressive, but Ilana was not impressed.

"I can't stand this!" she muttered to herself whenever she went about housecleaning. "Extra dusting, extra cleaning, rearranging all these rocks back into their places — it's ridiculous!"

As the days went by, Ilana's resentment grew. "I'm trying so hard to be a good wife to him," she argued to herself, "but if he really loved me and really cared about me, he'd be more considerate. He wouldn't bring home all these dirty, ugly stones."

But she could not convince Jonathan to change hobbies. And although he really wanted to help out with the extra work that they created, he never had enough time off to get to it before the accumulation of dust started getting on Ilana's nerves.

Then one day, everything seemed to go wrong. The car wouldn't start, so Ilana was late for her doctor's appointment and was forced to endure a horrendous wait. As a result, her mother-in-law was upset with her when she came late for their shopping date. When she returned to her car, she discovered a parking ticket on the windshield. On the way home, she remembered that she had forgotten to switch on the slow cooker, and supper would be raw. As she walked through the front door, an exasperated Ilana tripped on...a rock that had fallen from its place.

Ilana was fuming. She focused all her frustration on the man behind the rocks. The next hour, until her husband was due home, she was in a fury. She rehearsed again and again the lecture with which she was going to confront him. She made a mental list of all his faults and all the wrongs he had ever done her, and, of course, she readied her ultimatum concerning his rock collection. "He has a head of stone!" she concluded silently. "If he only cared about me half as much as he cares about his blessed rocks!"

As she stormed angrily about the living room, Ilana's eyes caught sight of a framed photo on the mantelpiece. There they were — a beautiful couple on their wedding day. Genuine joy and dreams of a happy future radiated from a smiling Jonathan and Ilana.

The smiling picture brought her up short. Ilana realized that she had lost control of the situation. That happy, caring individual smiling next to her in the picture — not the monstrous image she had invented — was the man she had married. Ilana pulled herself together. She showered, relaxing her tension. Changing into a dress which was her husband's favorite, she took a moment to dab on a touch of makeup. She was determined to greet the man she cared for with a smile and complete acceptance, knowing he would return that gesture in appreciation and love.

As she heard the car pull up, she hurried to the front door. "And to think," she thought to herself in amusement, "I was convinced my marriage was on the rocks."

Today, maintaining a positive approach is an enormous challenge, for contemporary society does not even regard homemaking as a worthy occupation. Rather, the career woman stands higher on the ladder of social success. Paychecks and tax returns are proof of her worth.

There is very little recognition given to the homemaker — who works extremely hard to do her job in an exemplary way. Rarely do women receive any formal training for this occupation, and they are certainly not paid salaries — the common standard of measurement — that reflect their worth.

Nevertheless, the Torah values above all the woman whose self-image is primarily that of homemaker. We should never think of our work in the home as something we are stuck with, or forced to do. Rather, by looking to herself, her family, and her home for creative fulfillment, she can find infinitely deep and meaningful satisfaction in her life. We are incredibly lucky people, given the chance to devote our lives to challenges within reach, the ones which can help us grow the most.

And the most critical challenge we face is overcoming the obstacles that are stopping us from being wonderful wives — like all the "incompatibilities" we are now *expecting* to find between us and our husbands. There are times when we run into some, and, being prepared for them, they are not nearly as annoying as they once had been. We can even smile about a few of them. But there are also the times when we come face to face with some particularly frustrating whoppers.

"Oh yes, we're different, all right," you hiss. "He's unreasonable! Impossible! He has an insatiable need to always be right. He's an absolute child with the maturity level of an eight-year-old. My anger and disappointment are justified. I'm sorry. *I'm* right and *he's* wrong."

When seeking to build harmony in the home, there is no such thing as *the* absolutely correct perspective. Coming from a stance of "right" and "wrong" — proving the other person's guilt — will only grant pyrrhic victories, where we win the battles but lose the war. We'll end up always right, but never happy.

This point is dramatically demonstrated by two cars at an intersection that both think they have the right of way. They can both end up *dead* right.

In one family it might be a sign of loving concern for a woman to remind her spouse to take a coat. In another home that might be interpreted as excessive interference. Where is there room for talking about right and wrong? It doesn't apply. The more one can truly enter the other person's perspective and try to see through the lens he uses to view the world, the greater the harmony that can permeate the home.

So, after recognizing the differences in our backgrounds and make-ups, we can more easily allow our husbands the right to their own perspectives. Let's try not to assume an attitude that our perspectives are the superior ones, even if we've always felt that they were — and still want to.

The advice we may have gotten from Great Aunt Matilda — "Train him right from the start" — is wrong advice. Accept him — don't try to change him. (He might change through your own loving example — but don't rely on it.) It will not be easy at all to accept all of our differences. We will have to keep on reminding ourselves again and again that there is often no right or wrong in individual perspectives and preferences — rather, there are only two people, who, by virtue of being human, look at the world through different lenses.

*   *   *

Given Avi's parents' careful attitude toward spending money, it was natural for him to go ahead and buy the cheap, generic tissue boxes instead of the finer name brand. When he returned from the store with them, Mindy said nothing, but silently she gritted her teeth. She kept in the nasty remark that was just itching to get out. What an effort! This was more difficult than any other test she had ever taken. She was still very far away from really accepting his style of spending, but the slightest dent had been made in her unyielding perspective on this issue.

*   *   *

We find in the Torah a description of what happens within us. When we manage to pry open a tiny hole — the size in a needle — G-d then opens an entrance for us, wide enough for a carriage to pass through. Once we make the gigantic effort to begin the process of granting our mate acceptance, the process actually feels like it's carrying us along after that. But it is still hard to start, so hard to make that first little needle hole of an opening.

How can we begin to accept our husbands as they are? First, by accepting that every one of us has a preconceived image of what we want our husbands to be. And we actually expect that our husbands are going to fit that mold (whether they want to or not!).

It has been said that a woman marries a man hoping to change him, and a man marries a woman hoping she'll stay the same. A woman's idea of marriage is often really her version of how she's going to "redo" him. Basically the man becomes another home improvement project. Although marriage is designed to help us fulfill our greatest potentials, we should not view marriage as an institution for the rehabilitation of our other halves.

The secret of domestic peace can be found in total acceptance, in realizing that our husbands are who they are, not our preconceived images of who they could be. And that even as they are, they can still become the ones we most deeply love.

Acceptance does not mean agreement. We do not have to applaud laxity in religious standards, laziness, indecisiveness, stubbornness and so forth. Acceptance means allowing our husbands the right to be themselves and *genuinely* acknowledging that they are the ones responsible for changing their behavior, not us. "Ahhhh!" we may be quick to retaliate. "But isn't that one of the most important aspects of a wife's job? To be a helpmate means to help him correct his problems. He needs me to point out his flaws and help him improve his character. He can't do that on his own. That's why we were put together! That's what I'm there for!"

Well, that sounds good. But does it also work that way? There are two crucial factors overlooked in this argument:

1) Judgment is the domain of G-d, not well-meaning wives seeking to better their husbands. We really aren't able to accurately judge other people. We don't ever get to see other people's final tally sheets, not even our husbands'.

And here's an extremely difficult one to keep remembering:

2) True change is impossible in an atmosphere of criticism.

Think of the people who had the greatest influence on us. Weren't they the ones who saw us clearly for what we were and didn't pressure us to be something we weren't, all the while still believing in our better side? The gift of acceptance creates joy and an exhilarating sense of freedom inside the marital bond. When people feel accepted for what they are, amazing things can happen.

Can't wait to get started accepting him? Let's just remember, no one ever said it was going to be an easy process. Acceptance goes beyond tolerance or resignation. It goes beyond an inward gritting of teeth and even beyond a begrudging putting up with his faults. But it may begin like that.

We are not meant to be perfect. We are meant to be ordinary human beings trying our best. And if we are struggling to move in the right direction, then any little bit that we genuinely try is a true achievement.

In order to be able to offer another acceptance, we need to be able to accept ourselves. And see how good it feels, being happy with who we are. If we cannot change or improve certain parts of ourselves, we can simply accept ourselves. And be realistic. Why put ourselves down? We can love ourselves. Creating a good, positive self-image is the only way we'll have the courage to really try to become even better.

In general, it's much more enjoyable to wear rose-colored glasses, not our black ones. All situations can be judged positively or negatively. With practice, it becomes easier and easier to view them in a positive light. It's very helpful to keep a list of our husbands' positive attributes (stored in our heads or on paper). We've got to throw away that nasty list of all the negative things that have accumulated.

Judging our husbands positively depends on what

colored glasses we choose to wear. Having a favorable outlook, seeing the cup as being half-full rather than half-empty, changes everything. Right this minute, it could be either "*Oy*! It's raining!" or "Oh wow! It's raining!" and either way those same wet drops are still coming down.

Let's say our husbands neglect to do something we had really wanted them to do. It can be extremely annoying. Or, we could try with all our might to pull out that valuable list we have stored away for an occasion such as this. The list that still has our husbands' positive attributes on it. Read it over again. He's still the same man that's described on that paper there; nothing has changed — even though he just did what he did!

We need to keep reminding ourselves that incompatibilities are not signals for despair. The challenge we have in life, and in marriage in particular, is to improve ourselves and our own behavior. We do not automatically adapt to one another, recognize our shortcomings or intuitively understand what makes our husbands tick. It's a long and interesting journey.

A wonderful thing to take along on our vital venture is that very valuable sense of humor. Being able to laugh at ourselves, not at others, can lighten all of our loads immensely. This doesn't mean self-deprecation or cruel sarcasm, but a good laugh can often break the tension and cheer up the atmosphere when we are getting carried away over petty matters. And one more thing we've got to have on our challenging "mountain-climbing expedition": a pack filled with patience to spend on our husbands, and on ourselves.

Can we ever meet this most demanding of challenges and come to really accept our husbands as they are?

There's only one way to achieve this: by being determined not to change him. That doesn't mean pretending to be a martyr and burying our negative feelings. But it also surely doesn't mean nagging, criticizing and putting him down. When our husbands are down, we don't need to push them down further. And we have to try never to compare them unfavorably to others. Doesn't it hurt incredibly deeply if they do that to us?

To walk the fine line of acceptance requires a tight-rope walker's exquisite sense of balance. We can expect to fall to one side or the other (wavering between a smoldering "martyrdom" and blatant fault-finding) many, many times. But with practice, we can gain this most precious skill and become adept at genuine acceptance.

We'll need this skill for the long list of idiosyncracies which we may need to accept. It could be that: he sleeps too much, he doesn't pay bills on time, he is often irritable, he is sloppy, he is stingy, he lacks confidence, he can't express his feelings, he isn't sensitive to yours, he is too loud, too introverted, he always leaves his things around just where you cleaned up, he is absent-minded, he is over-exacting and on and on. And this acceptance, eventually, won't even be granted begrudgingly! Imagine, if we keep working at it, the acceptance will really flow always more lovingly. It will come from an ever-deeper recognition of the other person (including your husband) having a right to be in this world, exactly as he is.

Let's look in on a part of one woman's uphill journey:

*   *   *

Libby was health-conscious, an ardent vegetarian cook, when she married Josh, a junk-food addict whose healthiest dinner choice was a hamburger with a bag of barbecued potato chips on the side. Although she knew this about him before they married, she had hoped that as he continued to sample her tasty health-food concoctions, he'd change his mind. He didn't. He became even more insistent on having red meat at every meal, snacking intermittently on a growing array of junk foods.

After a few months, Libby realized that he wasn't going to budge. She was deeply disappointed. The thought of their future children turning into junk-food addicts made her cringe. But he wasn't going to change. That was clear. So, after passing through various stages of grudging tolerance to a final real acceptance, she was able to completely let go of her expectations. She accepted the fact that she might have to spend the rest of her life cooking separate food for her husband and her children.

Libby began to cook main courses that catered to Josh's needs, with side dishes that would appeal to both of them. This went on for about a year. One evening Josh said, "Instead of the beef stew, could you make me one of your squash quiches for Shabbos?"

She said, "What? Wow! O.K.!" and went about looking in her recipe book for the dish he had suggested. Josh came over to her and said, "You must be so happy I asked for a quiche for a change, right?"

"For sure!" Libby smiled. "But I'd be glad to make you a meat-and-potatoes thing too, if it makes you happy."

Within a few months, Josh became as ardent a fan of vegetarian food as Libby, though now and then red meat and junk food did grace their table on special occasions.

Libby took the charge out of a long-standing conflict between them. An attitude of winning versus losing polarizes a husband and wife into positions of battle. Libby created an unpressured space for Josh, in which he simply decided to change his mind on his own. In order for anyone to make an honest change, it's got to be in his own time, in his own way, so it's *really* his own decision.

It is important to understand that this wife accepted her husband, not as a manipulative strategy to eventually win him over, but as he was, with a right to his own viewpoint, even if she still felt certain that her view was the better one. While it wouldn't have been ideal for Libby if Josh had stuck adamantly to his meat and potatoes, it still would have been genuinely acceptable to her.

Libby did not have expectations that her husband would come around to her view. And let us not get expectations from Libby's example. If we come to accept our husbands' presently irritating opinions and actions, it does not guarantee that they will eventually come around to our way of seeing and doing things. The only guarantee offered is that if we come to accept them, they will no longer be irritating. So either way, we will no longer wind up annoyed!

*   *   *

Here's a glimpse of a point on another woman's monumental "mountain-climbing trek" in her marriage:

*   *   *

Shani's husband caught a bad cold. Eli moaned and groaned around their apartment, feeling sorry for himself for days and not going to work. "Don't you even care about me?" he complained. "Can't you see how sick I am?"

She didn't think he looked too sick. She had been brought up in a home where you didn't take notice of little things like that. He was brought up in a home where he was put to bed for a week with every little sniffle.

Shani was pouring boiling hot water into the hot-water bottle Eli asked her to prepare for him, but some of the water spilled onto her hand instead. At boiling point herself now, Shani threw the hot-water bottle into the sink and stormed out of the kitchen. "I have had it with his feeling sorry for himself!" Shani fumed. "I'm going to teach him once and for all to stop being such a hypochondriac!"

But while marching toward their bedroom, ready to "give it to him," a funny thing happened. A little voice inside her asked, "Do you really want him to think that his mother was a better deal?" and she stopped in her tracks. "Will giving him a little bit of extra care and attention really harm him?" the voice continued. "And Shani, will it really harm you?"

Shani walked more slowly now to their bedroom and peeked in. There he was, just as she had left him, propped up with pillows, surrounded by tissue boxes, moaning. Shani forced a smile and made ten short words come out of her mouth: "Would you like a nice hot cup of tea, too?" Eli sat up straighter in bed and smiled back at her. A tiny opening, the size in a needle, had been made. And they were both feeling better already.

*　　*　　*

If acceptance enables our husbands to eventually change their behavior, fine. But if not, we will still have grown and gained immeasurably.

Acceptance, it is critical to remember, should never be used in a fraudulent way, as a manipulative device to achieve our ends. Let's not "act nice" to get some behavioral

change out of our husbands. We will probably be successful. But that should not be our underlying motivation. Let's
simply "act nice" so that we'll become more decent people.

Another type of manipulative acceptance to watch
out for is the kind granted begrudgingly and in a calculated
manner, part of an unspoken, but clearly understood bar-
gaining process going on between husband and wife. This
is when we expect him to tolerate our own whims, idiosyncracies and faults because we are tolerating his. One slip
up, though, when one partner doesn't keep up his side of
the "bargain," and a torrent of hurtful insults gets spewed
forth, suddenly unleashed from both directions.

To summarize: our foremost challenge, but one for
which we will never receive any public glory — not in the
form of awards, dinners given in our honor or even a small
salary raise — is the one that requires us to struggle to
accept our other half exactly as he is, instead of trying to
change him. We will be rewarded in relation to all the effort
we have invested, and the rewards received will be far, far
greater than those that could merely be propped up to
gather dust on a shelf.

It is important to note that there are ways, however,
for a woman to respond to a husband who is mistreating
her or acting dishonestly. It is foolish to come to accept
behavior that is abusive, demeaning or self-destructive. But
she will most probably need outside help in trying to rectify
such a situation. Reliable, Torah-guided counseling needs
to be obtained. And quickly. We should never be ashamed
or embarrassed to seek outside help for any problem, big
or small, at any point in our marriages.

The vast majority of people, though, change their
behavior in response to another person's compassionate
behavior. It is only a very small percentage of pathological

cases which cannot eventually respond in a normal manner to being treated with respect. The overwhelmingly common response is that the other person acts respectful in turn. The catch is, however, not to "act nice" in order to get an improvement to take place. Because then we topple off the fine line of acceptance, and our behavior slips into manipulation.

Eventually, we may find ourselves someday picking up those dirty socks he still leaves lying around and finding them...well, kind of lovable. We can see already that marital problems are greatly minimized by creating an environment rich in acceptance, and that a sense of security is a vital ingredient for growth.

Daily, our husbands confront a critical, high-pressured society which is nearly impossible to escape. With us, let them feel like they've entered a sanctuary. In contrast, let's provide welcome havens, offering what they need most — our acceptance.

FOUR

The Secret Language

The Talmud tells us about Rabbi Abba once followed a certain wanderer. The wanderer was tired and went to sleep in a very old and dilapidated house that was literally falling apart. Rabbi Abba was worried that the house would collapse on the man, so he sat down to watch over him that night.

Suddenly Rabbi Abba saw a huge poisonous snake approach the sleeping man to bite him. Before he managed to do anything, a wild animal came running out from the inner recesses of the old house and killed the snake. The wanderer peacefully slept on.

When the wanderer woke up and left the threshold of the house, it immediately collapsed. At this point, Rabbi Abba, unable to contain himself any longer, rushed over to the wanderer and begged him, "Please, please tell me. What are the good deeds that you have done which enabled you to merit the two miracles I just witnessed G-d perform on your behalf?" The man could think of nothing special.

But Rabbi Abba was not satisfied. He would not leave

the man alone until he could find out what good deed the man had done which merited such miracles. Finally, the wanderer said, "Well, all I can think of is that I never ever go to bed without making up with every person I may have hurt or offended in some way during the day."

"You are certainly worthy of such miracles!" smiled Rabbi Abba.

*   *   *

In marriage, there are bound to be interactions which lead to one partner, or both, getting hurt on occasion. Naturally, we try to develop our communication in order to reduce the frequency of these kinds of hurtful situations. But when our communication does not work, and we are unable to avoid a painful interaction, let's never forget the most basic lesson that this Midrash teaches us — to say, "I'm sorry." When we open ourselves up to ask for forgiveness, we will also feel ourselves worthy of Divine mercy. Then we will be open to accepting the Divine assistance that we need to continue building our marital relationships.

A healthy relationship is built on clear and honest communication. Listening, understanding and conversing all contribute to the empathy so vital to a marriage.

*   *   *

When Shoshana married Joseph, she thought they were both speaking the same language. They weren't. And little by little, she found this out.

Take, for example, the time when both Joseph and Shoshana decided to "spend an enjoyable evening together." What Joseph meant by that expression was a nice, quiet evening at home, sitting near each other, each involved in their own private pursuit. What Shoshana had in mind was going out for dinner and taking a long walk together afterwards. As you can imagine, it did not turn out to be a very enjoyable evening for either of them.

We need to expect to discover that although the words we and our husbands are using may sound the same, they often have widely differing meanings. What Shoshana and Joseph meant by the words "cleaning the house" and "spending a little money" were, well, not *exactly* similar. Even the simple word, "we," as in: "We need to take out the garbage," was not clearly defined. This became evident to both of them, also unpleasantly, as the garbage just sat and sat.

Understanding another person's language — the one they learned mostly at home, in their own unique environment, growing up — takes a long time. It is confusing when we don't know how to interpret another's messages. A lot of garbage gets left lying around.

If we come into a marriage, though, expecting to find that we are both speaking different languages — with different definitions for even the most basic things — we'll be more prepared for the challenge ahead.

Today, after twelve years of marriage, Joseph and Shoshana share a secret language between them that nobody else can really understand. But once in a while, they still find a new word like "soon," as in, "I'll do it soon," in which the meaning of the term isn't clearly defined and shared between them yet. Instead of having an argument about it, though, when the confusing culprit word is finally discovered, they both burst out laughing.

*　　　*　　　*

How can we progress from being unable to communicate with our husbands to being fluent in a shared secret language? The ideal of marriage is to come very close to one another.

This can only be achieved by listening to each other, talking openly, and trying to understand each other. When communication is broken, the chances of a happy marriage are lessened. Problem solving becomes impossible.

*   *   *

Elisheva once consulted a very wise woman because her marriage seemed to consist of nothing but an endless chain of arguments. She prepared a thick, black notebook filled with the many incidents testifying to her husband's faults and particularly to his quick temper.

The wise woman smiled at her sadly and said: "You really did your homework, but that's the wrong assignment you've got there."

She then proceeded to counsel Elisheva, suggesting various methods and alternatives to avoid constant conflict with her husband.

"Remember," she suggested at the end of their discussion, "a burning match will quickly burn out — but adding fuel will cause a fire."

*   *   *

There's no point leaving a broken telephone in our homes. Ignoring it and hoping it will go away won't do a thing. We may need to get help from a rabbi or a Torah-guided marriage counselor who can help us to fix the "broken telephones" in our marriages, if we have ones we've been trying to ignore, so that strong, healthy communication can be restored.

$$* \qquad * \qquad *$$

Judy and Benjamin were married for ten months. At first, they enjoyed a relationship of mutual affection. However, as the months passed by, and they each got busy in their professional lives, they began to sense a growing estrangement. Both of them felt the marriage lacked tenderness and warmth, but they were apprehensive about discussing their feelings openly.

They eventually decided to seek the advice of a rabbi. After discussing various issues with the couple, the rabbi suddenly turned to Judy, surprising her with a blunt question: "Do you love your husband?"

Judy stared at him, stupefied. "Of course I do!" she declared.

But Benjamin shook his head. "It's just not the same anymore," he insisted.

Judy was stumped. "But...but it goes without saying that I love you!"

Benjamin blurted out, "But I still need to hear the words."

$$* \qquad * \qquad *$$

While being very involved in making a living, it is easy to forget about what we are living for. We lose sight of the goals we most value, and we lose sight of the people we most value. Most of us are not even aware that an extra effort needs to be put into rising above that confusion, to keep putting our focus back on who and what means the most to us. Expressing love is something we are bound to forget to do when we get too wrapped up in things of much lesser importance. We get distracted even from our own feelings. The ones with the highest priority we don't take the time to express.

Although in Judy and Benjamin's marriage, it was Benjamin who verbalized his need to hear an affirmation of love from Judy, it is usually women who more often express this need openly. Women generally talk about feelings more readily than men. We usually have a greater need to hear words of affection again and again. That is why we may keep asking, "Do you love me? Do you really love me?"

Women generally express their feelings in words and expect words in return. Men, on the other hand, generally express love more easily through actions. If we take into account these common differences in communication styles, it may help us view our husbands' actions as a kind of language too.

Another difference between men and women that we learn in the Torah is that women, for the most part, have a more powerful ability to understand people than men have, since they were created with an extra dimension of understanding. This deeply insightful understanding is going to be the woman's main strength in overcoming the communication barriers in her marriage, and in helping her work together with her husband to develop a shared language that can make their life together more pleasurable.

Following are some of the important factors that enhance communication.

Attention

First and foremost, we must be interested in our husbands. This means looking at him, paying real attention to what he wants to say, concentrating on him and honestly listening.

*　　　*　　　*

Miri is talking on the telephone, having a very interesting conversation with her friend Lisa. Her husband walks in. She hasn't seen him all day, but she hardly raises her eyebrows in a sign of hello. She just goes on talking as if nothing has happened. He puts his things down and walks around aimlessly, still waiting for the hello, even if he isn't aware that he's wanting it.

Ten minutes. Fifteen minutes. A half an hour goes by. She still has not gotten off the telephone to greet him...

*　　　*　　　*

It would be wonderful if Miri could grab the opportunity to show her husband how important he is to her. All it takes is saying to her friend, "Excuse me. My husband just came home. I'll call you back." She, her husband and even her friend will gain from the experience.

If it's a long-distance caller, we could ask her to hold on for just a few moments so that we could say something to our husbands like, "I'm really sorry. I'll be with you in a few minutes." And then we should make every effort to curtail the phone conversation. We shouldn't treat him indifferently as if he were a piece of furniture. If an acquaintance walked in, we'd show her a lot more attention than that.

And once we've greeted him with welcoming smiles, hopefully we'll remember that, while everyone can talk, only true friends can really listen to one another. What our husbands are seeking from us is recognition, understanding and a compliment now and then. He's not craving advice. He already has a mother. You're his wife, and that's very, very different.

Openness

But what can we do if we're feeling angry at our husbands? We can either explode at him, or keep the anger inside and pretend it's not there, becoming a silent martyr as the anger grows and entrenches itself within us. However, there is another option.

In a healthy marriage, there are no secrets and no deceits. To be open and truthful with our partner is a great joy — and relief. This doesn't apply, though, in situations where the disclosures would be painful to somebody, like speaking badly about another person, or when our bluntness will cause our husbands sadness or anxiety.

*   *   *

Malkie prides herself on being a very honest person. So, being open, she tells her husband, "You know, you really look terrible. It's awful how fat you're getting!" That might be true, but it's hurtful. She may think she's getting the painful feelings off *her* mind, but really all she's doing is adding them onto his.

*   *   *

Careful Criticism

Criticism, especially when it is packaged as sarcasm, is cruel and unloving. It is never helpful to sit down and list for our husbands things we dislike about them, even if we deem the analysis completely valid. Only on certain very, *very* rare occasions should things be said that will undoubtedly cause our husbands pain. But even at those exceptional times, we've got to take great care to say what we have to say as gently and lovingly as possible.

Let's say we feel slighted and are anxious to pick a fight with our husbands. To avoid such a negative interaction, we feel we've got to express our hurt feelings to him. Or else, we realize, we will have to try to bury the anger, and then it will become a much deeper problem.

So first of all, let's choose the right time to express our feelings. When our husbands come home, for instance, we need to wait until they have eaten and are feeling more relaxed and available to us, before we "pop out with it." Remember this well: Let's *refrain* from expressing our feelings when our husbands are: 1) hungry 2) late 3) busy or 4) tired. We're doomed to fail if we forget to heed this warning!

The second thing is: let what's bothering us be the second thing. In other words, let's say something *genuinely* nice to him first, not to be phoney, or to catch him off guard, but for two much better reasons. Speaking pleasantly with him will force our thoughts and feelings to flow in a slightly more positive direction, and it will help him be more receptive to what we are about to say next. It's even better if our problem is the *third* thing we come out with, but for starters, let's be happy with stating our grievance secondly.

The third pointer for expressing negative feelings is: let's say *gently* what's on our minds. We can say what we have to, but let's try to keep ourselves in control. Our purpose is to convey as clearly as possible what is bothering us. That's what this confrontation is about — our feelings. Let's not demand change. We're not there to change our husbands. Let's just concentrate on our own feelings right then, not on how we want him to act differently because of how we are feeling.

Tenderness

Three things which are never helpful for us to do if we are really trying to bridge a gap in communication are: bearing a grudge, sleeping on a fight and competing with our husbands. A feeling of companionship is so much more pleasurable. When he's down, listen. Support him; don't ignore him. In a supportive atmosphere, we are able to resolve conflicts, or when that's not possible, to accept them.

Almost all marriages have difficulties because of problems that the partners have in communicating their feelings, needs and expectations to each other. This is a very intimate and personal type of communication. Really, it is as intimate as we can get. It's a far cry from the social but impersonal type of "How-are-you-fine-thanks-and-you?" style. There is really nothing in the Western culture that prepares us for the intimate relationship of marriage.

We need to have plenty of tenderness. We need to be open and receptive to our husbands. Why hold back from being the lovable people we really are? Let's be as loving to our husbands as we can. When we express feelings, they should not be mostly negative ones, like pain and anger. Let's make it a point to express many good feelings. A happy family expresses a lot of positive feelings to each other.

Men in the Anglo-Saxon world have much more difficulty expressing their positive feelings than we do. We can uplift our husbands' spirits through our appreciation and affection. And, whenever possible, we can express our good feelings about them through the clearest "language" there is. Before we leave each other in the morning, for instance, let's take several seconds off from rushing around to share moments of tenderness. It will make the whole day that follows immeasurably better. Why be stingy with expressions of affection? There is no shortage of them available to us. Let our lives together be as pleasurable as can be.

Clarity and Calmness

We're going to have to face it sooner or later — keeping up defenses doesn't work in marriage. It prevents us from getting close. Defenses are inappropriate barriers to have in our marriages. Let's be open, not guarded and fearful of expressing our feelings (in the right way, at the right time, that is), so that we can develop trust. Intimacy in Hebrew is "*yediyah*," which also means knowledge. Love is knowledge. And it never has to get boring. There is an infinite amount to learn about the men to whom we are married, and an infinite amount of intimacy possible between each couple.

And if we would like to be more open with our husbands, we can guess with whom we're also going to have to become more honest. Ourselves! We have to try hard to face our feelings, to be honest with ourselves about them and to understand them. The more clearly we understand our feelings, the better we can control both them and the behavior that follows from them. If we want to have the power to genuinely modify our feelings in order to make our lives happier, the first step is to face and accept those feelings.

*   *   *

Naomi was having a horrible day. Her hay fever was acting up, she was feeling overwhelmed with work, and then, to top it all off, her boss had insulted her. When her unsuspecting husband came home that evening, he noticed the important letter he had asked Naomi to mail for him that morning. "Why didn't you mail this letter?" he asked her. Uh oh...

Naomi exploded, somewhat because of her hay fever, somewhat because of feeling overwhelmed, but mostly because of the insult from which she is still smarting. It is her husband, though, who becomes the brunt of her vicious outburst. And since her husband also happened to have had a tough day...*uh oh!*

*   *   *

So let's first check that we understand our own feelings. Then we will be able to express them, instead of exploding unproductively and instigating an avoidable argument. It's also a good idea to try to find out what kind of day our husbands have had before we unburden ourselves. Living close with a person and not knowing the state of his emotions is like living with a time bomb. So in short, know our own feelings, let our husbands know them (except, as we discussed previously, when it is inappropriate to express them), and also try very hard to know our husbands' feelings.

There are different styles of communication from which we can choose:

1) Manipulating another — blaming, demanding, hurting, putting down, using sarcasm. This mode of communication puts the other person on the defensive, forces him to change or give up, and causes fights that get us nowhere and solve nothing.

2) Stating a message about our feelings as clearly and

calmly as we can. Afterwards, we may find it helpful to ask if he could repeat to us what he understood from our message, to see whether or not he heard correctly. Let him know if he got it right or not, and let that be the end of it. Or, at this point, with feelings clear to both, we can move on together to the third mode of communication.

3) Reasoning on an intellectual level — analyzing and diagnosing. This mode can lead to a decision as to what needs to be done. It is very useful, but as we know well, it is impossible to utilize when expressing negative feelings.

The second mode of communication works. It is effective, and it's an invitation to work on an issue. After using the second mode, we can use the third mode, which leads to resolving the conflict — decisions, suggestions, alternatives and compromises.

Dealing with Conflicts

Our effort has to be directed toward realizing and carrying out our own responsibilities, not toward educating and reprimanding our partner about the correct behavior expected of him. It's *much* easier to try to correct someone else. On our Sages' statement, "Who is a mighty person? One who conquers his natural inclination" (*Pirkei Avos* 4:1), the Baal Shem Tov commented, "The Mishnah states, '*his* natural inclination' — and not his colleague's" (*or spouse's*).

No marriage is free from many conflicts. And yet no one prepared us for them. Why did we think that once we got married we would basically live happily ever after, without putting a gigantic amount of effort into making it joyful? People think that a conflict is something ugly. But, in truth, it is a normal part of life that we should expect and try to actually see as an opportunity for growth that we have been granted. Our challenge, should we decide to accept it, is to use the conflicts creatively, to grow together, instead of apart.

Understanding Anger

This all sounds terrific. And it really can be. There's just one small problem. How in the world do we calmly and clearly state our feelings when it really seems like there's a bubbling volcano inside of us just about to erupt? Anger prevents us from using conflicts creatively. It is so powerful that it blocks off almost all the pathways in our brains, so that we are virtually unable to consider anything else but our one irate train of thought.

Anger takes hold of us when we are hurt or frustrated. Our heartbeats speed up. Adrenaline flows. Muscle tension increases. Many physical symptoms appear with it.

Anger is actually a survival tool, providing a surge of energy to deal with emergencies by fighting or running away fast. Usually, in our situations, however, anger is the result of frustration rather than fear. It's a feeling we needn't be ashamed of having. In fact, not being ashamed of it, and accepting it as a normal feeling, makes us much better able to subdue it sooner.

We are responsible only for what we do with the angry feelings we have. We have the power to control them. If G-d created anger, then He created the ability to control it too. We do not have uncontrollable tempers. If we are ranting and raving, it really is because we are allowing ourselves to do so.

There is a great misunderstanding that by giving vent to anger, we get rid of it. Actually, as research has proven, letting out our anger only intensifies it. This creates more anger, until a person reaches extremes of verbal or even physical violence. It's true that venting anger does bring some physical relief eventually. But let's not forget that it also angers the person to whom you are expressing your rage. Then there is more anger around to escalate the fighting.

So, what do we do with our anger, which is, as we said, a normal feeling? Firstly, do not suppress it. Bottling it up has a poisonous effect. Secondly, do not vent it. This, as we've learned, leads to more anger. (That burning match will cause a fire if we add fuel to it!)

O.K., then, what's left?

1) Acknowledge our anger to ourselves. Figure out *what* is really upsetting us. Once we have done this, we may find it helpful to delay relaying the angry feeling and first decrease some of its intensity by counting up to a certain number, taking a brisk walk, having a shower, or doing whatever else works for us to "cool down." A certain rabbi had a particular garment he would put on whenever he got angry — as a delaying tactic.

2) Communicate the state of our emotions without blame or accusation, without attacking our husbands for the feelings we have. Then our husbands will not have to get defensive (their adrenaline won't kick in, making things a whole lot worse).

3) Actually ask for our husbands' help in dealing with our anger. If there are any negotiations we'd like to take place, have them openly. Let's not bribe or try to punish our husbands in subtle or not-so-subtle ways. That creates a chasm between a husband and wife.

Finding Solutions

If we can manage to diffuse our anger, then the mood is set for solutions. These may be in the form of concessions, capitulation or compromise. Let's not sit way up on our high horses, waiting for our husbands to surrender. Let's capitulate as much as we are possibly able, and let's be honest where we're unable to capitulate any further.

Learning how to compromise, be flexible and forgive are all part of the educational experience of marriage. We are often too determined and adamant about proving ourselves right. Suddenly, justice becomes the issue that must be pursued at all cost. Is it really worthwhile, though? We end up proving ourselves right about the contested issue, but make everything else about our marriage quite wrong. After all, marriage is not a court case where one is challenged to prove the other at fault.

After winning our husbands' trust by being honest and trying as hard as we can to smooth things out between us a number of times, our husbands are very likely to accept or even offer compromise in the future. Compromise does not mean half/half. It could be any point along the line that you both could manage: three-quarters/one-quarter, two-thirds/one-third and so on.

If we can't reach a compromise — for example, he doesn't want to, or we just find it impossible to capitulate on a particular point — what can we do? Accept the fact and carry on just for the meantime. At least we now can see more clearly each other's viewpoints on the issue at hand. We have to allow our husbands their differences of opinion, even if we cannot go along with their views at the present. And while we take a break from discussing the issue, we can see if we can work on ourselves a little to get a bit more understanding of their perspective.

Marriage breakdowns are not usually the result of incompatibility, as we are led to believe. They are a result of the inability to make adjustments. An automatic understanding of our spouses is not one of the given characteristics of marriages made in heaven. There is no instruction sheet enclosed in the package (and handed out at the wedding), explaining in explicit detail just how each of our husbands' quirks and qualities goes well with ours, and how we need to specifically adapt to connect best. That's what we have to discover on our own.

Being Honest with Ourselves

Naturally, every marriage relationship has two viewpoints — ours and his. But it often happens that we see things only from *our* perspective, which means we focus on what changes we want *him* to make. In other words, how do we train him? If we could only focus on how to train *ourselves* to be better people, almost all of the problems that we have with others would wondrously fade away.

*   *   *

There was once a man who owned a detailed world map, meticulously hand-drawn and designed. He prized this fragile piece of art and kept it in a special drawer.

One day, on returning home from work, he discovered pieces of his treasured map lying all over the living room floor. After investigating, he quickly discovered the culprit, his four-year-old son.

In a rage, he reprimanded the son, lamenting the fact that it was much too complicated to tape the map back together. There was no way that all the tiny details could be put in order again. Full of anger, he stormed out of the room.

A short while passed, and the child excitedly called his father to the living room. On the glass cocktail table lay the map. The boy had put it together piece by piece.

The father was astonished. How could his son have succeeded where he surely would have failed? As if in response, the boy showed his father the back of the map on which someone had drawn a portrait of a face. The father laughed out loud as he understood his son's secret: he had simply put the face together, and all the pieces of the map fell into place.

*   *   *

Similarly, we have to first look to improving our own personal qualities. If this is done, many of the interpersonal problems in the marriage will sort themselves out more easily. The "marriage map" will fall into place.

*   *   *

Shira's husband is very late. Shira has prepared a beautiful dinner and already put it on the table. It is getting very cold. She puts it back in the oven to warm up. It is getting dry. Every now and then she checks the time. It is getting later and later. And Shira is getting more and more furious. Her anger is mounting, her thoughts are racing. "Where is he? How can he do this to me? We've been married only six months. He must be with some of his old friends..." Shira's imagination begins to run wild. Then Shira's husband comes in. What is she going to say to him? Very likely, it's a high-pitched, shrieking, nagging version of

"Where were you? Where have you been so long? I've been here waiting and waiting for you! What's the matter with you? Why didn't you phone? How can you do this to me?"

*　　　*　　　*

The first and maybe the hardest part of all is for Shira to really try to be honest with herself. Is she upset because her husband's dinner is now ruined? Is it *him* she actually cares about? She's upset because he let *her* down. The dinner *she* made got ruined. If she were concerned only about *his* welfare, she'd be delighted and tremendously relieved to see him. Honesty with ourselves about our needs — and our disappointment when our needs are not met according to our expectations — can clarify the situation and thereby diffuse potentially volatile interactions.

Could we imagine how different *and effective* this encounter would be if the next time it happens, Shira works on herself to greet him with a smile and a simple, "I missed you." She could do this only if she knows that she is shelving her bad feelings for a few minutes only, to diffuse the anger, and that she will express her feelings to her husband soon, at the appropriate time. Now she is free to concentrate, instead, on how relieved and delighted she is to see him finally.

What a dissimilar reaction she would get from him without his defenses up. And then, after awhile, when he is settled and relaxed and has most likely told her on his own what kept him so long, she could explain clearly and calmly how it made her feel to be waiting. They discuss it, but there is still a pleasant atmosphere pervading their home. That's it. The evening gets saved! And it is much more likely that it won't happen again very often, either.

We must remember that no problem is too trivial to discuss. Let's talk to our husbands, with intelligence, about what is bothering us about their behavior, for instance. And if it happens again, communicate again. If we see that something is coming from a very deep-rooted habit of his, perhaps discuss together the ways and means to try to get rid of it. But remember that uprooting a weakness takes many truckloads of patience, *at least*. Rav Yisrael Salanter said that it is more difficult to change just one character trait than to learn the entire Torah. Let's stop ourselves if we hear ourselves sounding any bit like a nag.

If our husbands are unwilling to try to improve, then forget about trying to make them willing. Instead, let's work on ourselves to capitulate or at least try to modify our behavior or the problematic situation. It's in our own best interest. Attempting to change one of our husbands' traits will almost always fail. And it will bring us tremendous disappointment and bitterness. The best thing is to get used to it and adapt ourselves to our husbands, with their hang-ups. It may seem to us that we are settling, but what we are actually doing is taking a giant step forward.

It would be enlightening, too, to work on changing our own annoying habits and traits. We may not be too successful at that either, but at least we'll get a much better appreciation of how close to impossible it is for anybody to uproot inherent or deeply rooted characteristics. We can search together for ways to overcome those kind of things, if both partners are willing. But we simply can't expect to uproot and change other people, not even our other half.

Encouragement

Rav Yisrael Salanter once spoke with a man who was not able to observe Shabbos because he was a heavy smoker. Rav Salanter asked him how many cigarettes he smoked a day, and the man answered, "Thirty-nine." So Rav Salanter said, *and really meant*, "Cut down to thirty-eight cigarettes only on Shabbos. Then you'll be observing Shabbos to the extent of that one cigarette you've cut out." The man was able to accept Rav Salanter's suggestion. He eliminated that one cigarette in honor of Shabbos. He continued this way until he was not smoking at all on Shabbos, and thus he was able to observe the laws of Shabbos fully.

*　　*　　*

Even a very marginal change is also a tremendous breakthrough. We've got to be extremely realistic with our expectations. Let's not *expect* improvement, but be genuinely encouraging with any minuscule step that gets taken.

*　　*　　*

Tami couldn't understand why her husband came home so late at night and left so early in the morning. She consulted their rabbi's wife. "What am I doing wrong?" she asked. "How come Ari is never home?"

During one discussion with Tami's husband, the counselor found out that every time he came home, Tami scolded and nagged him. Every time he had to make a telephone call, she had to know who it was and what they were discussing. She had plenty of critical comments, and basically, never left him in peace. Home was not a haven —

it was a very uncomfortable place for him. So he basically stayed away from it as much as possible.

It is for our sakes, as well as our husbands', that we should make our home a haven. When our husbands come home, let's remember not to immediately jump down their throats with all our problems and complaints. Never mind the broken washing machine and that he wouldn't take out the garbage that morning. Let's let him breathe a little at home, let him rest a few minutes, offer him a drink, enjoy his presence, give him a smile.

A smile, an encouraging smile, has an even greater effect on a person than food. The Maharal explains that we show honor to a person by smiling at him. It is tremendously energizing. And as Rav Moshe Chaim Luzzatto points out (*Mesillas Yesharim*, chap. 7), an external smile will bring about an internal smile, not only in our husbands, but within us too.

When we are not really in a good mood, the effort we are making outwardly will effect our insides, and our mood will be lighter. Also, if we smile at our husbands, they are *very* likely to smile back at us, and this will make us feel even better. It says in *Mishlei* (27:19), "Just as water is like a mirror to the face, so is the heart of man to man." And Rabbi Simchah Bunim of Peshischa explains the analogy in this way, "To see our reflection in water, we have to come close to the water and bend down." That is the same way to enter the heart of our other half.

Pointers

Here are a few pointers we may find very useful in learning how to fight effectively. Or maybe by now we should just call it getting over disagreements.

1) One couple's solutions are not necessarily good for another couple. Every couple has their own way of dealing with disagreements. In other words, your friend's resolution to her "in-law issue" may not be successful in your very different marriage.

2) Let's try very hard not to raise our voices, even if our husbands do. And also let's try hard not to interrupt him. After we have explained as unemotionally as we can exactly what got on our nerves, for instance, let's really give him a chance to explain, if he wants to, why he did what he did. Let him get his thoughts and feelings out as fully as he would like.

3) Keep the argument local. In other words, when we are trying to resolve a particular issue, let's not start thinking about all the other annoying things our husbands do. Let's not bring up what happened last week, last month or last year. We need to keep the discussion to the point.

Putting these last two points together means, therefore: Let's not get hysterical *or* historical.

4) Make every attempt possible not to focus on who is right and who is wrong. Our homes are not courthouses. They are places in which to bridge differences. The less expectations we have about marriage, the happier we will be. If we are not focusing on "What's in it for me?" and "I'm not getting this and I'm not getting that," what we do get will be appreciated and enjoyed more fully. Let's express this thought to ourselves whenever we are being overwhelmed by feelings of disappointment, and see how it helps.

5) Remember that arguing is normal. Somebody who

claims that she never had a disagreement with her husband has either a tendency to lie or a very short memory. But still, we need to make every effort not to argue in front of our children. When we are having a disagreement, if nothing else, it's at least a chance to get to talk alone together.

6) Let's try to be first to make friends again. Jump *off* our high horses. It's lonely up there. We can learn from what we teach children. Let's be first to apologize about some aspect of the disagreement. Let's swallow our pride. Then we'll be able to speak more lovingly. It won't make us into lesser people. It will make us into greater people. We can say we are sorry about something we genuinely are sorry we did. And try to end on an encouraging rather than a discouraging note. Make peace. We've got nothing to lose from taking this action and everything wonderful to gain.

7) When we are upset with our husbands and we won't get the chance to see them for awhile, instead of letting angry feelings build up within us, it is very helpful to write them down. Even if we're only going to read these descriptions to ourselves and then tear the paper up, writing down what is in our hearts helps to remove the tension that's building up. We may even find ourselves laughing after we read over our compositions, suddenly realizing that we were making a mountain out of a molehill.

Shared Language

A well-known rabbi once got a call from a couple in the midst of a heated argument. The call came at midnight, and the wife involved said it was an emergency. The rabbi rushed right over to their apartment.

When he got there, however, the couple shame-facedly admitted that the argument had been over who should take out the garbage.

And it had finally been settled. They had just gotten momentarily overwhelmed by this mundane molehill.

Why had it felt like an emergency to them only moments before? The task in question had evoked feelings in each of them, and they had not yet developed a common language with which to explain them. And so with neither one being able to hear or understand what the other was saying, the volume had been turned up considerably high, until it felt like an ear-shattering emergency instead of a simple discussion.

*   *   *

In an argument, there can be a situation where both partners feel they are right, each from their own perspective. Or it could be that we just can't stop feeling that we are the only ones right, and our husbands are *clearly* wrong. The question then becomes, What is more important to us: winning this argument, that argument and the next one, or making peace in our homes? Naturally, there won't be anything to argue about if there is no home. And when there is no peace in a home, it's not much of a home.

Marriage breakups actually start when partners try to win little arguments over things like who will close the window or take out the garbage. Then the battles grow. So we have to keep putting things in perspective. Agreeing on an acceptable resolution and making peace in our homes is much more of an achievement than winning a little argument — or even a big one for that matter.

Communication is vitally important in the beginning of a marriage — and the beginning is as long as the beginning lasts — until the basis for a shared secret language has been established. After that, it is still immensely valuable because our relationships can *always* be improved. Where there is good, there can always be better. Let's set aside time, in a nice atmosphere, just to talk to each other, about big things and about little things too.

*   *   *

Sima has been married just a few weeks. She comes home after a very exhausting day working in a hospital. She's uptight, with a very tense, drained-looking face. What she really needs is her husband's shoulder to cry on. She just wants a little encouragement from him.

But just as she sits down to talk with her husband and starts unburdening her misery, there's a knock at the door. Her face suddenly lights up when she sees her neighbor, who has come by with the two grocery items Sima had asked her to pick up. She greets her neighbor in a very friendly, cheerful voice, but when she closes the door and turns back to her husband, the big smile is gone. In its place is that same tense look again. Her husband is furious!

"For her you have a big smile, but *me*? All I get is a sour face!" he growls. "I guess it's clear who you care about more!" He cannot understand, at this point, that she wants to unfold her real feelings only to one to whom she feels close, and that revealing her true state to him is a sign of intimacy, not a lack of it.

*   *   *

A man is not created with special mental telepathy to read his wife's mind. Very often women complain, "Why didn't he know how tired I was and offer to help me out for awhile? Couldn't he tell how exhausted and overwhelmed I was?" We do need to talk and say what we are feeling. Even better, we should talk before it becomes a very intense feeling. Let's not harbor resentment against our husbands because we think they should have realized how we were feeling on their own without our having to spell it out for them. Tell him directly, pleasantly, and with the biggest smile we can manage at that overwhelming time.

Marriage is not meant to be a guessing game. There is no need ever to make our husbands feel like losers. Are we feeling tired? Let's say so. Are we feeling depressed? Let's say so. Let's make it easy for him to know our emotions — *and that includes the good ones.*

*   *   *

When Man reached the moon for the first time, the Ponivitzer Rav was asked for his opinion on this feat. He answered, "How great is Man, and yet how small. How great — he can even reach the moon. Yet how small — he cannot even reach the heart of the man standing next to him."

Prove your greatness by reaching out to the man standing closest to you — your husband.

*   *   *

What does all the discussion about having constructive disagreements have to do with sharing a secret language? Shared secret languages don't appear magically. They unfold in a way that is far, far better than magic. Each time we break through some confusion and conflict which is keeping us distanced from our husbands and reach a new understanding, our own totally unique language is being formed. At first it will be awkward, as all new languages we learn are, but as more and more conflicts arise and get cleared up, the secret language that is shared will begin to flow in a wonderful way.

FIVE

The Enormous Value of Peace

There was a great Sage by the name of Rabbi Meir who used to give a lecture every Friday night. A certain woman used to attend on a regular basis. One Friday night, the Rabbi spoke longer than usual, and when the woman arrived home the door was locked. Her husband, angry with her for coming back so late, had locked her out. She went to stay with her neighbors, and there she remained for several weeks.

Eventually, the neighbors went with her to see Rabbi Meir. It seemed the angry husband had demanded that he would only let her back in if she spat in Rabbi Meir's eye, as he claimed it was the Rabbi's fault that she had come late.

Rabbi Meir saw through Divine inspiration why they were coming. When they arrived, he asked if there was anyone who could do something for his sore eye. The woman went forward, and he told her to spit in his eye seven times, and then it would get better. After she did his bidding, he said to her, "Go back to your husband now, and tell him: 'You told me to spit in Rabbi Meir's eye one time, but I did so seven times.'"

The woman went home, and there was peace between that woman and her husband from then on.

The students of Rabbi Meir were very upset, however. How could their revered rabbi allow such a disgraceful thing to be done to him? Rabbi Meir answered them: "Let not the honor of Rabbi Meir be dearer than the honor of G-d, Who desires most that there be peace between a husband and wife."

*   *   *

Our Sages do not justify in any way the husband's despicable behavior. Their message to us is that the value of peace, in G-d's eyes, is *enormous*. This is illustrated by the extent to which the honored Sage was willing to sacrifice his personal dignity to obtain peace between a husband and wife. In fact, the power of peace is so great, the Torah teaches us, that it is thanks to peace that the world exists (*Maalos HaMiddos*).

What is peace? The Hebrew word for peace is "*shalom.*" *Shalom* comes from the word "*shaleim,*" which means "whole." Peace is the bridging of opposing forces. The husband and wife, as two halves, become one, a whole. This is peace.

Since our marriages were made in heaven, we are ideally suited to our husbands. "G-d made for him (Adam) an *aizer kenegdo*, a helpmate opposing (balancing) him" (*Bereshis* 2:18). The Netziv explains that every wife has the corrective ability to be just the helpmate to her husband that he needs, according to every tiny nuance of his personality. Every wife is so suited to her husband that she has the potential to be constantly of help to him. A husband and wife have the ability to be perfectly balanced with each other, and *because* of each other. The wife is suited to helping her husband with every one of his character traits. That includes the negative ones too. She is ideally suited to bring out his full potential.

*   *   *

Michael has a terrible temper. He can flare up at the smallest of things, like a misplaced pen, and start shouting, slamming doors and throwing things. Michael's wife, Leah, could, if she's just reacting without really thinking first, shout right back at him, "What's the matter with you? Why do you have to always scream at me? What an awful temper you have!"

It may look like Leah's being a help to him, trying to get him to control his temper, but if she hasn't put careful thought into figuring out the best way to deal with this problem, then chances are she's not being much of a help at all.

If Leah feels hurt and put down, taking every one of his angry outbursts very seriously, she will be needing help too. But if she recognizes this character flaw for what it is from a position of strength, with her womanly wisdom, she may come up with a strategy combining tact and diplomacy to help him reduce or overcome his problem.

The best way for her to deal with Michael's temper would be to think of it not as the problem of Michael, the stranger, but as a problem that Michael, her other half, has. They are still two halves of one whole — *even* when one half misbehaves.

If she remains calm, she may be able to help him calm

down eventually. How? By speaking softly and soothingly, and honestly empathizing with him. Through using tremendous loving wisdom, she can act as a true helpmate to him. Only in a peaceful manner will Leah achieve change.

*   *   *

To be successful, a woman needs to get to know well not only her husband's strengths and weaknesses, but also her own strengths and weaknesses. A husband needs to be able to trust that his wife really has his interests at heart. As *their* problem, not *his problem alone*, it can be handled together. If we are fulfilling all our obligations as wives, only then can we even consider the issue of how best to help our husbands with a particular problem. Otherwise, all our efforts will be futile. We will not be trusted as true helpmates. Every woman has a sixth sense, her womanly intuition. This wisdom has great depth. We can use it creatively to affect changes in a patient and positive manner.

We should never assume that changes made in either ourselves or our husbands will be "all or nothing" transformations. Some changes take days, some take months, some take years and years, and some things can't be changed. But the only way there is a *possibility* to help ourselves or others improve is by not criticizing, by being pleasant and focusing on the positive, by being attentive, by behaving diplomatically — and by constantly searching for even better ways to deal with the issues.

When our husbands do things that upset us, instead of being critical, let's take a little time to think of what would be a more effective *and* more loving thing to do. The time put into thought will be worthwhile. If we just make an off-the-cuff response we are only going to alienate our husbands and increase the distance that keeps partners apart. Let's take the time to think before we act. It's a great habit to develop, especially when it concerns what means the most to us. And if we need help thinking clearly about a good approach to a problem, we should go out and seek qualified, Torah-guided help.

Let's strive to forget about the *I* and *you.* It is only *we.* Even when he was the one who erred, let it be *we.* Regarding our husbands' negative personality traits as we would physical ailments can be helpful to us in handling them in a thoughtful way. For example, if a woman had a husband with a heart problem, she would not dream of shouting at him because of it. She would not blame him for the condition. So, if she remembers that "changing one personality trait is harder than learning the whole Torah" (Rav Yisrael Salanter), she can relate to her husband's temper problem the same way. It involves acknowledging that there is a problem, and then trying to determine the best methods for handling it, treating it and also living with it forever, if need be. From this position of clarity and strength, she will be functioning as a true *aizer kenegdo.*

The same as a husband's heart problem might take weeks, months or years to improve (if at all), so emotional problems (like temper problems) may take weeks, months or years to improve (if at all). If both the husband and wife are working on the problem, while both are standing on the same side of the fence, they will have double the strength to work on it. And any slight modification that might eventually be obtained is a tremendous achievement.

*   *   *

Yaffa was put in a difficult situation when a close family member attacked her for her husband's unfriendliness to him. Yaffa really used her intelligence in dealing with the situation. First, she excused her husband's behavior, saying that perhaps he had not been feeling well at the time. Then, rather than attack her husband for being rude, she calmly discussed the problem with him at an appropriate time.

"*We* have a problem with my brother-in-law," she opened the discussion, "How do you suggest we should handle *our* problem?"

*　　　*　　　*

When one half of a whole is weak in any area, either temporarily or even permanently, it's the other half who must take over for the two of them. The reward for the two (the two halves) is greater than it would have been if just the one (the one half) acted alone (see *Koheles* 4:9). If one spouse slips up, the other can cover for him, raising him up in the process too.

*　　　*　　　*

Penina was about to explode at her husband for not taking out the garbage...*again!* "Why do I have to do *everything* around here?" she fumed. This time, as soon as her husband got home, she would *really* "give it to him," she decided — once and for all.

Unable to keep all that hostility inside for another half-hour until he got home, Penina took down a big box of Lego for her children to play with. Then she went to take a quick shower, which managed to cool her down, in more ways than one.

Feeling much calmer, she reached out for a little prayer. It was a prayer for her husband's well-being that she kept tucked away. It put her back in touch with the deeper reality that peace in her home was more important to her than the place of the garbage.

She felt ten feet taller before her husband got home. She had done the right thing, and she knew it. Penina had gotten rid of the garbage, in more ways than one.

*　　　*　　　*

"We" as a married unit can be moving toward functioning at full potential *even if* the wife is the only part of the unit doing what feels like all of the growing. A woman can't lose anything by growing. Each of us has an infinite amount of work we need to do on ourselves, regardless of what our other half is up to. And we are here in this world to keep becoming better human beings, regardless of whether those around us notice that we are.

We may feel that nobody notices the changes we are struggling to make within ourselves, but that is really not the purpose of people around us. *We* will notice, because suddenly we will feel in harmony with our natural essence, and that is enough. Or, as we develop more reverence for our inner core, it will *become* enough. We need to have more respect for the potency of our own minds to generate our internal happiness.

If there are a few things a woman wants to improve, either in one particular half of the marital unit or the other, she should gradually tackle each challenge one at a time, in order of priority. Too much, too fast, can be too large an undertaking. Let's not try and effect changes in many areas at once, but only one at a time — thought through well.

Wives have such a tremendous urge to correct their husbands, but it is very difficult to do this properly. It should be attempted only very rarely, and only when a wife is fulfilling her sphere of responsibilities toward her husband, and always with great wisdom.

No one likes to receive rebuke and get told off — even in the nicest way. We don't. And our husbands don't either. So, it's just not worthwhile to focus on faults. We should keep looking, rather, for good things, and then we can use encouragement, which we don't have to use sparingly. It's a much more enjoyable way to help a person overcome faults — though it also requires intelligence, especially focusing powers, to implement. Ignoring as many faults as we can and helping a person to feel good about himself is still the method of choice.

Our Sages teach us that a person needs to have a *good eye*, on the lookout all the time for the good things in others. We can see the good things if we want to see them. We are more likely to notice positive acts we ourselves do, and the good traits we have. Therefore, when we see our husbands as our other halves, we are better able to see their good traits and actions too.

It will be of enormous benefit to us, as no one likes to be reprimanded. We know *we* don't like it. And neither do our other halves. And if we ever do deem it absolutely necessary, let's keep in mind the wise advice of Rabbi Chaim Friedlander: "A person is like a diamond, and one should wipe the dust off it, not with a hard brush where the bristles create tiny scratches in the diamond — not with criticism. Wipe the dust off a diamond with a very, very soft brush — with encouragement — and then the diamond will shine brighter from day to day."

Even if the outcome is not as we'd like it to be —

which is often the case — as long as we are doing our utmost, we have nothing to feel guilty about. We get reward for the effort. Any positive action taken is never futile; the reward lasts forever. It is good to keep in mind that what we need to be concerned about is our "next world" and our partners' "this world," not vice versa. So even if the results of our efforts are not seen so quickly, we should realize that this is not the only place where our efforts get seen. Our reward in heaven is guaranteed.

Let's slightly revise an old saying and remember that, "Home was not built in a day." Achieving true peace in our homes will be a lifetime project. Sometimes it may even seem like we're going one step forward and then one step backward. That is fine. We are human beings, with human weaknesses.

Peace and harmony in a home does not mean that there are never conflicts. If we are growing and changing in life, there will always be conflicts. Harmony doesn't at all mean stagnation. It means that there is a connection between the two parts of the whole. And the more the connection grows, the more harmony there will be in the home. As Rabbi Shlomo Wolbe explains, peace comes in the bridging of opposing forces. Throughout our married lives we can keep on improving this unity, merging more and more deeply into our state of wholeness, truly becoming one.

Creating a good atmosphere in our homes demands that we devote our intellectual skills and creative talents to our homes, so that our minds will come to align with our hearts. The radiance present in a wonderful Jewish home does not stay contained there; its glow spreads far and wide.

By struggling to conduct ourselves properly, we are fulfilling our obligation to G-d, as the purpose of life is that all that we do should be for the sake of heaven. The efforts we put into creating peace in our homes is, foremost, the fulfillment of the will of G-d.

"A man cannot be without a woman, and a woman cannot be without a man, and both of them cannot be without the Divine Presence" (*Yerushalmi Berachos* 80:9).

When a woman prays to G-d to help her to create unity and peace in her home, her efforts will ultimately attain not only peace, but also the scent of Gan Eden. The couple's joy will be like the joy between Adam and Chava in the very first marriage, and the Divine Presence will reside in their home (*Sheva Berachos*).

We are fortunate to have a partner in G-d, to Whom we should pray to help us succeed in building united and peaceful homes. *Shalom bayis* does not mean that there will be no disagreements, but that there will be an overriding sense of peace and harmony in the home.

The results of our efforts are so far-reaching, we cannot even imagine them. As our Sages teach us, "When a person makes peace in his home, it's as if he is making peace between every person in the Jewish nation" (*Avos DeRabbi Nasan*). In other words, the unity between a husband and wife in a Jewish home has such a powerful holiness that it has an effect on the totality of the Jewish People. In fact, the effects are on the whole wide world. "*Shalom* is so great that the entire Torah was given in order to establish peace in the world" (Rambam, *Hilchos Chanuk-kah* 4:14).

Prayer for a Wife to Say for Her Husband

יהי רצון מלפניך ה׳ אלוקינו ואלוקי אבותינו שתשמור
ותנצור את בעלי מכל נזק מכל רע ומכל חולי. ותתן לו
חיים טובים, חיים ארוכים, חיים של כבוד ועושר. ותתן לנו
זרע בר קיימא ובנים הגונים וצדיקים. ותטע בינינו תמיד
אהבה ואחוה ושלום ורעות. ותקבע אהבתי בלב בעלי
שלא יחשוב בשום אשה בעולם זולתי ויהיה בעלי שמח בי
יותר מכל הטובות שיש לו בעולם. ותטע בלבנו אהבתך
ויראתך לעשות רצונך לעבדך כיהודים כשרים ותמשיך
עלינו קדושה וטהרה במחשבה דבור ומעשה לעשות
צדקה וחסד עם עמך ישראל ותברך את בעלי ברכה
שלמה ברב עז ושלום כדבר שנאמר יברכך ה׳ וישמרך יאר
ה׳ פניו אליך ויחנך ישא ה׳ פניו אליך וישם לך שלום
ונאמר ה׳ ישמרהו ויחייהו ואושר בארץ אמן כן יהי רצון.

May it be Your will, Hashem, that You watch over my
husband, and keep him safe from all injury, from all harm
and from all illness. May You grant him a good life, a life of
honor and good fortune.

Bless us with living seed — righteous children. And
plant between us love, friendship, respect and peace forever.

Instill love for me in my husband's heart, so that he
will never think about any other woman except me. May

my husband find more happiness with me than with any other pleasure he has in this world.

Plant within our hearts love and fear of You so that we will fulfill Your will and serve You as good Jewish people.

Enwrap us with holiness and purity of thought, speech and action, so that we give generously and perform kindnesses with Your people.

Bless my husband with a full blessing, with strength and with peace. As it is written, "May Hashem bless you and keep you from harm. May Hashem shine His face upon you, and grace you. May Hashem lift His face to you, and grant you peace."

As it says, "Hashem shall watch over him and keep him in happiness in His world." Amen. May this be His will.

From Chuppas Chasanim

SIX

The True Meaning of Love

In the Talmud there is a story about two brothers who lived on opposite sides of a mountain. The younger brother was married and had a large family. The older brother had never married and lived alone.

Every night the single brother would rise at a quiet and late hour, gather a big sheaf of wheat and carry it over to his brother on the other side of the mountain. He said to himself, "My poor brother has so many children and demands upon him — and so little livelihood. Let me at least ease his burden somewhat by giving him from my portion."

The married brother also would rise in the dead of night and transport a sheaf of wheat to the hut of his single brother. *He* thought, "My brother lives alone, with no one to help him or to gladden his heart. Let me at least ease his loneliness by providing him with extra sustenance. Maybe in this way his heart will be lighter."

Every morning when the brothers awoke they were amazed to see that their pile of wheat had not diminished during the night. This went on for years and years. Then one night the brothers met as they were crossing over the mountain with their sheaves of wheat. The brothers looked at each other in astonishment, hardly believing their eyes. Realization suddenly dawned on them. They embraced with deep emotion, each recognizing the sacrifice of the other in the secret exchange that had been going on for years.

The Talmud continues by telling us that when G-d looked down on this mountain and saw the love of these brothers, He decided to build our Holy Temple on that very site.

*   *   *

A home is likened to a mini-Temple. G-d dwells where there is love between a husband and wife. *Love!* The most abused word on earth. The way we usually use it is in commonplace expressions like, "I love pizza!" But if we really and truly love the pizza so much, why do we eat it all up and make it disappear? When we consume that slice of pizza, what we are doing is loving ourselves, not the pizza.

Love, as we all know, is an emotion. How then can we be commanded in the Torah to love? We are instructed both to love G-d (*Devarim* 6:5) and to love another as we love ourselves (*Vayikra* 19:18). We learn one from the other. First we need to love ourselves (which includes our internal selves, not just our physical selves), then we need to love another, and through this, we are learning to emulate G-d, coming closer to Him, and growing in love for Him.

Still, if love is an emotion, how can we be commanded to love? The answer can be found in the word itself. Love, in Hebrew, is *"ahavah."* *Ahavah* comes from the root *hav*, which means to give. Love comes from giving.

If we give to another individual, he becomes part of us, and we can come to love him as we love ourselves. The starting point, though, is loving ourselves, as otherwise we're incapable of loving another. If we love the G-dliness in ourselves, we can love the G-dliness in another, since all people are created in the image of G-d.

People love those things to which they have given. A farmer loves his crops. A builder loves his house. An engineer loves his bridge. They see their efforts in that to which they have given. The way to promote love in our marriages is to find many opportunities to show our husbands that we care about them.

A wife tending to her husband's needs, a mother awakening to respond to her crying infant during the very early hours of the morning, a woman opening the door of her home and heart, generously inviting a guest in to eat — all are acts of giving that enhance our lives, as well as the lives of our husbands and children, with far-reaching ramifications.

By giving, by doing for others, we become closer to them and begin to love them. The purest love in the world is the love between a mother and her infant. The fact that this individual is completely dependent upon her, and that she is almost constantly giving to this new little person, makes her love deepen very quickly.

Pure love does not depend on external factors. If love depended on a particular condition, when the condition would cease to exist, so would the love (*Avos* 5:16). Pure love depends on the giver, not on the recipient. This is a really mind-expanding concept to grasp. True love does not expect anything in return. It is a wholly altruistic feeling, where the pleasure is in the giving, not in the taking.

Love between husband and wife is a unique type of pure love, an emotion that cannot be understood in terms of other feelings. It is a G-d-given gift to the world to bring man and woman together in a way that will enable them to give the greatest pleasure possible to one another. Love is the foundation of the family, and, therefore, it is the foundation of the whole world. On *chesed,* on the basis of kindness and giving, the world was built. If we understand that love means giving, and opportunities for giving are endless, then through giving we can move toward a love so great it is limitless. In marriage, since the opportunities for giving are limitless, it follows that our marital love has the opportunity to be limitless.

The Torah tells us that man and woman were originally created as a single androgynous unit (*Bereshis Rabbah* 8:1). G-d then separated the unit into two distinct individuals. Husband and wife began as a single entity, and this oneness is their natural state. The love that builds between them from marriage is a result of their natural tendency to become one again (see *Bereshis* 2:24).

When love between a husband and wife grows very deeply, they become like one person. This is demonstrated in a story told about the Tzaddik of Yerushalayim, Rav Aryeh Levin. Once when he went to a doctor with his wife, he told the doctor, "Her toe hurts us." Although the toe was hers, the hurt was clearly felt by both of them. When our partners' stubbed toes feel like they are *our* stubbed toes, there are no barriers that cannot be overcome.

In the Talmud, we find a man's description of the relationship that he had with his wife: "When the love between us was intense, we could have dwelt together on the edge of a sword" (*Sanhedrin* 7a). And the intensity of their love would even overpower the pain from the sword, making it negligible. The Talmud goes on to explain further, however, that when a marriage is not a loving one, the whole world is not big enough for that couple.

We can learn the process through which love grows from the Torah's account of Yitzchak and Rivka's relationship. We read, "Yitzchak married Rivka; she became his wife; he loved her" (*Bereshis* 24:67). It does not state that he loved her and then he married her. How different this is from the pervasive attitude which sees marriage as the culmination (or, more often nowadays, the beginning of the end) of a couple's love. From the Torah's perspective, love begins only after marriage, because true love comes from a form of giving in which there is no holding back, within the safe, though expansive, confines that the marriage commitment provides.

Through giving, we draw closer to someone. When we are closer to him, we get to know him better, recognizing more and more of his inner virtues. And then we want to give to him even more and deepen our love further. So, according to the Torah (*Bereshis* 18:8), we acquire love through increasing our knowledge of someone, not by accidentally "falling in love" with him.

Contrast this Torah view with the scenarios that are daily played out in the press: Movie star X or royal prince Y or famous millionaire Z pursues the girl of his dreams, covergirl A, soap opera star B or top rock star C. With the world envying them and desiring to emulate their dazzling spectacle and upcoming bliss, they are married. Not much later, the headlines begin: "He Battered Me!"; "She's a Drug Fiend!"; "He's Unfaithful!" The romances have shattered. Only their lawyers are left smiling happily ever after.

How do we achieve a genuinely great love with our

husbands? By doing for them, by getting to know them, and thereby, becoming ever closer to them. On the simplest level, by preparing the food our husbands like, going to places that our husbands enjoy, having over guests they enjoy, doing the things they like us to do and trying our best to please them. For sure, love sounds a lot easier when we're just talking about it theoretically. But finding out everything he wants and then trying to do all these things for him — that may seem *genuinely hard!*

And on top of all this, we need to be concerned about fulfilling our husbands' need to be respected and admired.

*　　　*　　　*

Joe came bounding up the stairs and into the apartment, virtually brimming over with some news that he couldn't wait to tell Toby. But Toby was engrossed in *the* most exciting part of an incredibly suspenseful novel.

She did manage to emit a grunt or two in his direction, "Hmm? Yeah? Uh-huh..." But she was clearly not really paying attention. Her indifference — no matter how fascinating the climax of that novel was — would have insulted anyone.

*　　　*　　　*

First of all, we need to give our husbands our attention and respect. By listening to our husbands, complimenting them and showing them that we care about them, we demonstrate that we admire them. Trying not to show them indifference, interrupt them or embarrass them are ways of showing them respect.

*　　　*　　　*

They had a houseful of guests, since it was her parents' wedding anniversary. Chana decided this would be a really effective time to "show off" her broken dining room chairs and maybe finally get something done about them.

"As you know, my Shimmy has two left hands. He can't fix a thing!" she laughed. And everyone else did too. Even Shimmy. But inside, Shimmy felt very embarrassed. He had tried to fix them several times, always unsuccessfully. He felt even more humiliated, somehow, though he didn't show it, when his brother-in-law immediately offered to fix the chairs for them.

*   *   *

And let's not forget *appreciation*! Why let our husbands look for it under *A* in the dictionary? Let's give it to our husbands every day, in generous doses.

*   *   *

Shulamit was tired so she went to bed early, leaving a huge pile of dishes in the sink. When she got up the next morning, the sink was empty. Aaron had washed all the dishes. She immediately called him at work to thank him for his kindness.

*   *   *

The more we communicate our gratitude, the more our husbands will want to do for us. But let's not express our thankfulness *for* that reason! Concentrating on the magnitude of blessings our husbands have brought into our lives will also help us overcome the feelings that may sometimes plague us about giving more than we are getting.

The True Meaning of Love | 109

Instead of taking our husbands for granted, even for the small details we would easily miss if we didn't make a concerted effort to notice them, let's see how much more grateful, and therefore, gratified, we can become.

*   *   *

"You have such a terrific memory!" Alisa smiled, as she watched her husband plop the groceries down on the kitchen table. "I can't believe how you remembered to stop off and get some tomato sauce for dinner."

*   *   *

In the humdrum of daily life, it's easy to forget these essentials for a happy marriage: complimenting, listening to, caring for, admiring and appreciating our husbands. These things provide them with the attention and respect they need and deserve. And what do we need to remind ourselves *not* to do? — interrupt our husbands, embarrass them or show them indifference.

Let's make it a point to compliment our husbands at least once a day. If we haven't done it by the time he is going to sleep, let's do it then! If we aren't used to it, just know that it's one of those things that is *only hard to do at first.* Giving our husbands a sincere compliment will become a joyful experience for both us and them.

*   *   *

Ettie liked to do the bedrooms first and leave cleaning up the kitchen for last, a job she never managed to get to on busy mornings. But one day she remembered that Issy really preferred a tidy kitchen to an orderly bedroom. She struggled to put her own personal preference aside and changed her "morning rush" order of doing things.

*   *   *

Let's try very hard to adapt to the way our husbands would like things done. It's especially good to ask our partners what they'd like us to do for them whenever it is not clear to us, and let's try to really put effort into appreciating all that they do for us. When they are talking to us, let's *actually stop talking* to the children, our neighbors or those on the other end of the phone, and *listen to them.* Everyone will learn something very valuable from doing that.

*   *   *

Ruth heard her husband's car pulling into the driveway and quickly unplugged the phone. She wanted to make it clear to him, to herself and to anyone else that might try to intrude into their limited time together that her husband was more important to her than anyone or anything else.

*   *   *

Let's not dress to make an impression on guests, the doctor or the people we will meet while shopping. Let's dress to please ourselves, *but also our husbands.* We can be comfortable and relaxed at home, but still make an effort to look attractive when our husbands are with us.

*   *   *

There was once a very wealthy man who lived in Jerusalem. Then he lost his business and all his properties and was forced to move into a very poor section of town. In order to provide for his family he had to work very hard doing manual labor he was unaccustomed to — fixing old, broken doors.

Then every evening at exactly the same hour, the neighbors began to see the man's wife leaving her house, all dressed up. They would all whisper behind her back and secretly laugh at her. "Doesn't she realize that her dressing up days are over?" they would ask. "Who is she trying to impress anyway?" they would wonder.

But one day all their laughter ceased. They gained a deep and great respect for this woman when the reason for her actions was finally revealed to them.

The woman's husband used to return from work very tired and depressed, since he was not used to being poor and having to work at such a job. So in order that he should be in a better mood when he came home, his wife decided to try to lift his spirits by dressing up for him and waiting for him downstairs at his workplace. Her greeting him there like that and their walking home with her smiling face beside him was all that he needed to enter his house in an uplifted mood.

*   *   *

Women sometimes slouch around the house in a robe and slippers all day, but when they go outside, even just around the corner, they dress up from head to toe. For whom? The gas station attendants and bank clerks couldn't care less how they look. But their husbands? — to them, it really *does* make a difference (see *Tanchumah VaYishlach* 5). Small efforts are sometimes the greatest acts of giving.

It is worth spending just a few moments making ourselves attractive for our husbands. Those are moments well invested. Simply greeting them affectionately when we see them will have a tremendous effect on the marital relationship, as every act of giving increases love.

*   *   *

It wasn't always easy for Tzippy to find a quiet moment in her home to spend together with Saul in the morning. One child or another always seemed to have something pressing to say. But Tzippy always made the effort, even after twenty years of marriage.

*   *   *

Our life together is too precious to take one another for granted. Those few moments before a couple part each day can be extremely valuable ones. And even when we are physically apart, little gestures can be incredibly meaningful.

*   *   *

"Hi, Gershon!" Hinda said, calling her husband at work. "I know you're surprised to hear from me at this time in the morning, but there's nothing to worry about. And nothing I need you to get this time either! I just was thinking about your warm smile right now, and I felt like calling and telling you that I'm so glad I'm married to you!"

*   *   *

The story is told of a king who could not find happiness, no matter what. His favorite dishes were placed before him. Jugglers were brought to amuse him. But all efforts made on his behalf were to no avail. The king stormed out of his palace in complete frustration and went for a long, long walk, searching for happiness.

He walked and walked until he came to a forest, and there, deep in the woods, he came across an old man, sitting and weeping. The king asked him what the trouble was and he answered slowly, "My poor wife is very ill, and I do not even have the means to buy her the medication she needs. I don't know how to help her!"

The king took off his crown and extracted from it one of its jewels. He then handed this precious stone to the old man. "Go in peace now, and buy your wife the medication she needs. May she recover quickly!"

The old man was overjoyed to be able to help his wife. He thanked the king profusely and asked him, "Your Gracious Majesty, what could I ever do for you in return?"

The king replied, "You have already given me what I wanted. You have made me happy." The king smiled. "No greater reward could I expect!"

*   *   *

In our lives, we can find out quickly that the habit of giving promotes happiness and satisfaction. Here in this world, the reward for giving clearly is happiness for the giver. But, in truth, our reward lasts forever. It lasts through this world and into the next. The happiness that comes from giving lasts an eternity.

*   *   *

A man once had a dream in which he was shown what would be in the World to Come. First he was shown the punishment of the wicked. He saw a banquet hall in which people were seated at tables laden with the finest, most mouth-watering food. Observing the people, he was horrified to see that they were eyeing the delicacies hungrily, yet they were miserably starving. Why weren't they eating?

Upon closer observation, he noticed that their hands were tied to knives and forks which were three feet long, too long to bring to their mouths. They could not help themselves to the food — it was so close, yet out of reach — and they could think of no alternative but to go hungry.

The man was then shown the reward of the righteous. To his amazement, he found them sitting in the same banquet hall at tables with the same setting. Their hands were also tied to long cutlery. However, they appeared well fed and content.

Those who merited to sit at these tables were accustomed to giving and benefiting others. They quickly realized that by feeding one another across the table everyone would be satisfied.

*   *   *

The basis upon which a marriage stands is a willingness to give — to give and give and give — without expecting anything in return. Again and again, though, our thoughts will probably stray to "What about *his* side of the bargain?" and "Just what do *I* get out of this deal, anyway?" As soon as we can hear those thoughts coming through clearly, we've got to take hold of them and throw them far out of our minds. Thoughts like, "Why doesn't he do the same as I do for him?" appear valid, but they are actually insidiously destructive, making the foundation of the home more and more shaky the longer and stronger they persist.

If we are wondering whether our husbands will get accustomed to just taking if we are always giving to them, we can reassure ourselves that that is not the way humans tend to operate. Are we afraid that if we give too much our husbands will take advantage of us? That they will "use us"? That is a very common assumption, but a very limiting, downright deadening one. And it's also incorrect. What we need to understand clearly is that very few people will respond negatively to being treated with respect and compassion. Most people are not made that way, to take without giving. If our husbands receive from us, eventually they will give, even double and triple what we've given to them.

When we are feeling "unloved," the mode of action, rather than wallowing in self-pity, is: *do more for him*. The more we do for our husbands, the more of ourselves we will be putting into them. And as each of us becomes more and more a part of the individual who is our other half, our love for him will grow and thrive.

*   *   *

Leora went back to the teacher with whom she had studied marriage before her wedding, complaining about the sad state of her relationship with her husband. "He simply doesn't love me anymore," she said. "Maybe he never really did." After several sessions, the woman gave her a list of things to do for him: ten different ways to give to him every day!

Leora looked at the list and balked. "What's the point of all this?" she asked. "It won't make any difference. He really doesn't care for me anymore."

But her teacher persisted. "Let's try it and see what happens," she said. "You do these things. Come back next week and we'll see what the situation is."

One week later, Leora arrived at the woman's home, all excited. "Well, I don't know what happened," she said, practically squealing, "but he's acting so much nicer to me now. So I don't need counseling anymore! I guess it was a mistake that I came here to begin with. How do you like that? My husband really does love me after all!"

*   *   *

Sometimes just demonstrating clearly to our partners that we are willing to be giving, and willing to forgo, to act in our husbands' interests, rather than our own — *although it's difficult* — may make *all* the difference in the world to them.

A husband and a wife each have different tasks and characteristics that complement one another. The Chazon Ish compares them to the right and the left hand, which complement one another and work together. We need to be less concerned with looking out for our own particular benefit and measuring for equality. It is so much more energizing to be focused on the common goals we share — our deepest priorities in life — and let these help to unify the differences that come between us and our partners.

In marriage, we are uniting not only two bodies, but also two souls which are incomplete without the other half; yet each part has no demands upon the other. The majority of a woman's characteristics — physical, emotional, intellectual, spiritual — are there to be utilized in her marriage. All the love and warmth within us can find its outlet within marriage. Each and every husband needs his wife's specific and unique qualities. G-d created every husband to be able to give to his wife what she needs too. But the power to release the flow of love from him is in the wife's hands. A woman has the most tremendous influence on her home, through every small word that she says and action that she does.

The prevalent philosophy now teaches us that our personal rights come before anybody else's. This is not the Torah view. And it is difficult to rid ourselves of this selfish way of approaching life. All too often, marriages break up from very trivial conflicts that have grown monstrously, unnecessarily. "If my needs aren't met, this gives me the right to be nasty to him and see that *his* needs aren't met!" We hear this self-centered approach all too often. This is a grave error. Two wrongs don't ever make one right. Life is not necessarily easy, calm or glamorous. Life is G-d's gift to us. G-d owes us nothing. But we have the ability to maximize the use of our lives to the utmost levels.

Jewish wisdom teaches us that the reward is in relation to the effort. We often have to make sacrifices for others. This is what it means to be a mensch, a real human being. Giving to others enables us to genuinely grow and become better people. When we give to others, especially to those closest to us, we save ourselves from becoming egoists, and we also develop our own potential.

We have to keep putting our priorities in order, because it is very easy, otherwise, to get them all mixed up. Our marriages are more important to us than careers or social obligations, but too often this gets forgotten. If we keep refocusing on the fact that our marriages are of top priority, then we can try our best to act accordingly.

*   *   *

Gavriel didn't have enough money to buy a bouquet of flowers for Shabbos, so he used to bring home one rose for his wife every Friday afternoon.

One *erev Shabbos*, however, he arrived at his doorstep with rose in hand, only to find there a delivery man carrying the most tremendous and magnificent flower arrangement he had ever seen. Debbie had been doing some charity work for the local school, and this was a gift to her for her many efforts.

Gavriel felt suddenly silly holding his one little rose next to this breathtaking array of flowers. Imagining his wife not caring at all about his one rose when she would open the door and see that exquisite arrangement, he was about to make a hasty retreat from the doorstep, ready to toss his single flower away. Just then Debbie opened the door.

Walking right past the astonished delivery man, who was holding the gorgeous flower arrangement, Debbie made a beeline straight to her husband. "What a *beautiful* rose!" she exclaimed, just like she always did.

*　　　*　　　*

Currently predominant views notwithstanding, we still believe that first come our obligations to those close family members to whom we have made a commitment, and then come our own personal wants that do not clash with these family obligations.

*　　　*　　　*

Avigail had put in a lot of effort to prepare four-course meals for two very special guests who were invited for Shabbos.

Then Dave came home late Thursday night, feeling awful because he'd had an extremely difficult week. "Please, Avigail," he said, "could you postpone the guests until next week? I just don't feel up to having company this weekend."

"*What!* After all my preparations! How inconsiderate you are!" These were the kind of thoughts that immediately rushed into Avigail's mind, but she struggled hard to catch them before they came out, and she forced a smile.

"No problem," she just barely managed to say. By the time she had packed away all the food she had made into the freezer, she was surprised to find that she already meant it.

*   *   *

Real life isn't always easy or pleasant. But if we take a few deep breaths, roll up our sleeves and have confidence in our G-d-given abilities to raise ourselves up through trying circumstances, we can genuinely grow. Avigail undoubtedly gained more from struggling to rise above her initial disappointment and to respect her husband's feelings than she would have had the weekend gone on as planned — even if one of her intended guests had been a self-improvement seminar instructor!

First and foremost come our responsibilities as wives — to really try to respond to our husbands' needs. Marriage is not a hindrance at all to personal growth. On the contrary, it is a hindrance to selfish, egoistic desires running amok.

So giving to our husbands can take a wide variety of forms. From giving words of encouragement, which is like giving water to a wilting flower, all the way across to forgiving, not hanging onto our hurts, talking it out, then reaching out, forgoing and forgetting. What bad can possibly come to us from giving of ourselves in the most real way possible? We won't lose ourselves by giving of ourselves. It's the way to find more and more of our inner resources — and to come closer and closer, in fact, to emulating the Ultimate Giver of all, namely, G-d.

A marriage struggling to grow is like a masterpiece waiting to be revealed. There is a tremendous potential waiting to be brought forth. And what we will achieve with our marriages depends on what we are determined to achieve, the amount of effort we are willing to put into it. Let's not settle for a dull existence together, or live in a fantasy world, dreaming. We can go for the real thing. Let's not hold back. Let's give — and really live!

SEVEN

The Key to Unity

When Moshe Rabbeinu came to build the Mishkan (Tabernacle) in the desert, he asked *bnei Yisrael* (the children of Israel) to donate their most valuable possessions for the Mishkan. The women came forth, donating their copper mirrors.

What was so valuable about these copper mirrors? When these women had been slaves in Egypt, their husbands, due to their severe suffering, had stopped having intimate relations with their wives. But the women had intuitively realized that this was not a positive step. "We will not be enslaved forever," they thought with certainty. "G-d will eventually save us." And so they devised a plan.

As slaves, they lacked the most basic tools to make themselves more attractive to their husbands. But from tiny pieces of copper put together, they managed to make for themselves small mirrors. When their husbands returned late at night from their harsh slave labor, feeling degraded and exhausted, both physically and spiritually, they were not inclined to be intimate with their wives. But the women, having used their mirrors to make themselves attractive, brought their husbands food and drink and encouraged them to renewed hope.

Ultimately, this act on the part of those courageous women is the reason given for *bnei Yisrael* being saved. As it says, "In the merit of the righteous women, the Jewish people were saved" (*Sotah* 11b).

We also know that the holy cleansing vessel (the *kiyor*) in the Mishkan was later made from these same copper mirrors. When Moshe Rabbeinu was at first hesitant to accept these mirrors that the women wanted to donate, he was told by G-d, "Take them! These are more dear to me than any of the other donations to the Mishkan" (Rashi, *Shemos* 38:8).

And we know that the *kiyor* vessel in the Mishkan, made from these copper mirrors, was used to create peace between husbands and wives. The Maharal explains further that because the women showed their desire for intimacy with their husbands, even under such adverse conditions, they then conceived and later gave birth to children who were truly worthy of redemption (*Gevuros Hashem*, chap. 43).

*   *   *

So we can see that intimacy between a husband and wife is a holy endeavor which G-d Himself had to explain to none other than Moshe Rabbeinu! If even Moshe Rabbeinu could have a misconception about this most intimate of human activities, it is clear how the world at large, on a *far, far* lower level of understanding, could be *glutted* with gross misconceptions. The Jewish view has always been a far cry from the non-Jewish approaches, which have ranged from the worship of physical pleasure as an end in itself to the condemnation of physical intimacy. The latter view was epitomized by the asceticism of the early Christians and others, in which this subject was seen as an expression of man's sinful nature.

In stark contrast stands the Jewish view that there are three partners involved in the conception of each individual human being: G-d, the father and the mother (*Niddah* 31a). If there were something "dirty" about this act, how would G-d be involved in it, as our Sages say? As the Ramban explains: "G-d did not create *anything* that is intrinsically disgusting or ugly. Know that the act of union is a holy and pure matter when carried out in the right manner at the right time and with the right intentions. A person should not think there is anything degrading or unbecoming in the act of union, G-d forbid" (*Iggeres Ha-Kodesh*, chap. 2).

We see that the physical union between husband and wife fulfills the purpose of marriage, which is "they shall become one flesh" (*Bereshis* 2:24). It is, in fact, an entrance door through which holiness enters into the home. The Divine Presence dwells in the home whenever the couple expresses their love for one another in this ultimate way, striving to achieve the maximum closeness available between two human beings.

The only prerequisite to this is the couple's observance of *taharas hamishpachah.* This system is one of the most basic tenets of Judaism, in which there are certain divinely decreed times, based on the woman's own natural rhythms, when husband and wife are not permitted to each other physically. This interlude of separation from the expression of physical closeness culminates with the use of the *mikveh* preceding the beginning of a new period of physical intimacy.

Taharas hamishpachah is the prerequisite that sanctifies a couple's physical reunion. It is a *chok*, which means that the reason for this commandment is beyond our comprehension. Still, as our Sages explain, the separation periods clearly serve to enhance the physical reunion, so that when a couple reunites it should be as exciting as it was on their wedding night. As it is written, "So that she be as dear to her husband as at the time of their marriage" (*Niddah* 31b). (The details of this most vital of mitzvos and insights into its observance may be found in my book, *The Secret of Jewish Femininity — Insights into the Practice of Taharat HaMishpachah.*)

*   *   *

Miriam was pouring out her heart to the rabbi's wife. She had been to numerous counselors, and after many hour-long sessions, nothing had so far been of any help at all to her shaky marriage. The rabbi's wife listened intently until Miriam had finished speaking and then asked, "Is all well between you in the bedroom?"

"There is nothing there," responded Miriam. "How can there be? Doesn't there first have to be peace in the living room?"

*   *   *

This attitude is a very common one, maybe because it sounds like common sense. But it does not take into account the mystical elements involved in this unique expression of closeness between husband and wife which was given to us by G-d.

The numerical equivalent of the letters in the Hebrew words for love, "*ahavah,*" and one, "*echad,*" is thirteen in both cases. And if we add the values of the two words together, we get the number twenty-six, which is the numerical value of G-d's name. This symbolically expresses the Jewish view on intimacy. As we learn from the *Zohar*, it is the fulfillment of the ultimate goal of marriage, which is to unite the two bodies who share two half-souls, so that they become "one body, one soul."

This extreme closeness, therefore, *has the power* to help a couple overcome their differences. It gives them the strength which emanates from a one body, one soul unification. They become no longer two separate individuals, but rather one, handling their difficult challenges together. Therefore, it is actually a grave error to assume that only when a couple is "at peace in the living room," and only then, is there place for creating peace in the bedroom.

We can see this concept expressed in the broader context of the Jewish wedding ceremony itself, as the marriage is really considered to have become a marriage only after the couple has united physically. "But they hardly know each other!" we may think. "Aren't they still just two strangers?" we may ask ourselves. And yet, G-d decreed this to be their first step together, as it is this "becoming one" in fact, which will have a positive effect on their relationship in the living room, the kitchen and any place in the whole wide world.

The closer the two partners get, the more united their two halves become, the stronger will be their bond. And ultimately, this will give the couple the strength to overcome their many differences and learn to adjust to one another on all fronts.

"But if I am feeling distant from my husband, how do you expect me to be intimate with him?" That's a popular question. Clearly, a couple cannot be intimate while they are quarreling. They *would* need to work out their dispute beforehand. This is a halachic prerequisite, in fact. It is definitely a challenge to struggle to rise above both our petty grievances and our more serious ones, but we can do it. We can either try to work them out immediately or shelve them to be dealt with another time, in order to allow ourselves the chance to grow closer to our partners in this G-d-given manner that promotes healing.

In fact, the living room will be much easier to straighten up, once we have the bedroom in order. The first step in putting our bedrooms in order is, as we've mentioned, the observance of *taharas hamishpachah*. The second step is understanding that the closer we are able to get, the more holiness will pervade our homes. G-d is one, and when a couple becomes one as they are meant to become, then G-d can put His Divine Presence in their union. Therefore, the closer they are, the holier the union. The key to a couple's unity is in the bedroom, which is compared to the Holy of Holies chamber in the Beis HaMikdash (*Melachim* II 11:2). As the Holy of Holies is the most sacred place in the Temple, so is the bedroom the holy of holies in our homes, which are likened to small sanctuaries.

Clearly, when we think of the couple's union as being an opportunity for the Divine Presence to enter our homes, we will find that excuses like "I'm too tired," "too uptight," "too this" and "too that" will be much less frequent. It is our attitudes which determine how we function. When we remember that it is an opportunity to cement our relationship, we will be loathe to forgo the chance to do so.

*   *   *

Sara felt she was trying her best to make her marriage work. "I'm always willing to do my husband a favor and be intimate with him," she explained. "But how many favors do I need to do?"

* * *

Sara really may be trying her best, but she has simply not yet understood the meaning of marital relations. She could learn from her namesake, Sara Imeinu, our first foremother. It is written that one of our very great Sages once entered the *Me'aras HaMachpeilah,* the cave where Avraham Avinu and Sara Imeinu are buried, and saw Avraham sleeping in Sara's arms (Maharal, *Chiddushei Aggados* 3:82).

Husbands were given the commandment of *onah,* to give their wives physical pleasure. As the Raavad explains (*Baalei HaNefesh, Shaar HaKedushah*), this mitzvah is regarded as both a need and a pleasure of women. Clearly then, a woman should not be thinking she is doing her husband a favor by having intimate relations. Rather, it is a favor to herself and to her marital relationship.

And G-d wants us to *enjoy* fulfilling this commandment. As the Ben Ish Chai has written about it, "Although a person has to have intention to fulfill G-d's commandments, he also has to have desire for this with all his heart" (*Torah LeShmah, Ohr HaChaim* 72).

G-d clearly wants us to feel like fulfilling this mitzvah. Just as we feel a desire for food, which connects our bodies with our souls, so do we need desire in order to connect our two bodies and our two half-souls. We can see that G-d created our digestive systems in such a way that we first smell and taste the food we need to eat in order to live. In other words, we get to derive pleasure from eating. If there was no pleasure derived, we would actually be loathe to partake of food. Similarly, G-d created us in such a way that there is pleasure in the physical union, since otherwise we would try to avoid partaking of this activity. That would have a negative impact on us, on our husbands and even on our children.

There is a difference in just two letters between the Hebrew word for man, "*ish*," and the Hebrew word for woman, "*ishah*" — the letter *yud* in "*ish*" and the letter *heh* in "*ishah*." And when these differences are combined together, they form G-d's name. When a husband and wife express their closeness, and their differences merge to become one body and soul, the conditions are met for G-d's Presence to dwell with them too (*Sotah* 17:1).

Creating such a unity is clearly not a one-sided arrangement. Rather, it demands that both partners be involved. As the Ramban explains, "She should also join with him in holy and refined thoughts. Then their minds will be fused as one, they will both be united momentarily, and G-d's Presence will rest between them" (*Iggeres HaKodesh*, chap. 5).

The physical relationship is referred to as "the mitzvah of *simchah*" — the mitzvah of joy. It needs to be done with joy. And if the woman's involvement with marital relations is with joy, it brings joy into the home as a result.

We can comprehend the reason for this if we recognize the mystical element involved. Our marriages were made in heaven, and yet we live down here on earth, with all of the many challenges this involves. The key to connecting heaven and earth, and the key to the connection between body and soul, is this holy act which attains full unity between a couple.

They become one via this "mitzvah of *simchah*." We can attain the greatest spirituality via our physical bodies.

This is the basis of Judaism, which shows us how physical pleasures are uplifted and sanctified.

The unity and love expressed in this G-d-given manner creates the highest and most complete place of holiness in the world. And to reach it, we simply have to work on enjoying this intimacy.

Our foremothers, we are told, had relations with their husbands for their pleasure (*Tosfos HaRosh* on *Horayos* 10b). As explained, the true connection between husband and wife cannot be obtained without pleasure, "since if she does not enjoy this, she will not cleave to him" (Rashi, *Sanhedrin* 58a). And then the purpose of marriage — which is to cleave to one another (see *Bereshis* 2:24) — will not have been fulfilled.

Therefore, the woman's goal should be to enjoy this intimacy with her husband. Her pleasure will, in fact, be his pleasure too, this being the nature of the universe. A woman's natural inclination is to be loved by her husband. And, as Rashi explains, this means specifically in the intimate area of their lives (Rashi on *Bereshis* 3:16). "It is known that a woman's fundamental hope in life is that she will have a husband who loves her," said the Steipler Rav.

Especially when our lives are very busy, we need to know clearly what the Torah view is on this subject, so we can make it a top priority in our lives. We can then remind ourselves that the key to happiness in our married lives is not dependent on washing every last dish or baking X amount of cakes. It is based on being true wives and achieving the closest expression of love possible.

G-d has given the ability to every woman to know how to be a real wife. She just needs to be willing to use her mind and energies to access those abilities. Some preparation in mind and body is usually needed, just as preparation is needed in order to fulfill any other mitzvah.

The unity between husband and wife is referred to as the mitzvah of *simchah.* The Rema explains that the greatest joy comes when we resolve our doubts. Therefore, the best opportunity for resolving our doubts about whether or not our marriages were made in heaven, comes out of deepest knowledge of the other person. Thus, the Hebrew word for knowledge, *"yediyah,"* also has another meaning — marital relations. This is the expression of our utmost knowledge of one another, involving the total giving of one to the other without holding back. In this situation there are no doubts that the two are one.

As the *Zohar* says, "When a married couple kiss, their life breaths (*ruchos*) come together. When they embrace, then their spirits (*nefashos*) come together. And when they have marital relations, their bodies (*gufim*) come together. This situation, when they are totally one body, one soul is one of real happiness. And we also know that G-d does not dwell in a place lacking joy. The Divine Presence resides only in a place of happiness. So now we can comprehend even more deeply why, if there is a lack of desire between two partners, there is a loss of holiness in their union. As the Ramban says, "If they are together without great love and desire, the Divine Presence does not reside there" (*Iggeres HaKodesh,* chap. 6).

Clearly then, the woman's goal has to be to infuse her relationship with her desire. A woman who makes herself attractive to her husband so that he pays attention to her (not through coarse verbal means or force, but in the Jewish manner, modestly and playfully) will see the positive effects of her behavior on the next generation. This is a reward that is promised in the Torah (Tur, *Orach Chaim*).

The woman's challenge is simply to use her G-d-given

tools to make time and devote energy to being a real wife. G-d helped the generation of Jewish women wandering in the wilderness to make themselves attractive to their husbands. Together with the manna, G-d sent down many different kinds of perfumes for all the forty years they were there (*Yoma* 65a). Every woman is created with an extra dimension of understanding. She has the ability to learn her particular husband's likes and dislikes, and light the lights of peace inside her home. The Shabbos candles are the symbol of the Jewish woman's ability to rekindle her husband's love (*Zohar*).

The holiest things are hidden from the public eye, as exposure to the outside world would cheapen them. That is why this subject is a very private one. This most holy of topics is not for casual conversations between women. It belongs to the private lives of each couple.

Tznius, modesty, is the covering of the good, the holy, the beautiful. Our crown of glory as Jewish women is our modesty. All of our femininity is reserved for our husbands. So, though a woman's modesty is a basic tenet of Jewish life and it is most praiseworthy, her behavior with her husband in private is not a contradiction to this in any way (*Sefer HaMiddos LaMeiri*). In fact, the more we abide by the Torah in modest behavior, whether in dress or actions, the more we are protecting ourselves from connecting with other men, and the more we are enhancing our exclusiveness to our husbands. Then the more precious, holy and pleasurable our union can become.

EIGHT

Of Kings and Queens

We can learn about kings and queens from the sun and the moon.

"G-d created the two great lights — a great light to rule by day and a small light to rule by night, and the stars" (*Bereshis* 1:16). The Midrash points out the apparent contradiction in this verse. Initially, it states "the two great lights," which makes it seem that they are equal in stature, and then it refers to them as a great light and a small light with the stars. The Midrash resolves this by enlightening us as to the sequence of events.

After being created equal, the moon approached the Creator and said, "Two kings cannot share one crown." G-d responded, "Go then, and reduce your light, and I will give you the stars as compensation" (*Chulin* 27b).

*　　　*　　　*

Man and woman were originally created as one being (*Eruvin* 18a). By originally creating husband and wife in a single entity, G-d invested a man's nature with the capacity to fulfill the commandment of marriage, "and he shall cleave to his wife" (*Bereshis* 2:24). In other words, he would cleave only to his wife and not to another woman (*Sanhedrin* 58b). Then G-d put man to sleep and created woman as a separate being from him, and she was called an *ishah*, because she was taken from *ish*. And G-d describes her as a helpmate opposite him, his *aizer k'negdo* (*Bereshis* 2:18).

When they were separated as two distinct beings, the couple's relationship could be compared to that of the sun and the moon. The moon, who for the sake of peace dimmed her light, was rewarded with all the other stars shining beside her. The wife who elevates her husband to the position of king, thereby making herself into a queen, is likewise rewarded for doing so with peace in her home and shining little "stars."

And just as the sun and the moon complement one another, so do the husband and wife complement one another. Both are of equal importance, but are not identical in their roles.

Man and woman were created as two different human beings. Each was delegated a role in accordance with his or her nature and capabilities. Within a marriage, these roles are complementary; each one enhances the other. But for this to occur, each partner must first learn to respect and appreciate his or her mate's different nature and responsibilities. A man and a wife complement each other when they both fulfill their own particular obligations.

Respect for one's partner's tendencies and role will facilitate the proper understanding so vital to a marriage. The relationship will thrive, and the couple will surely enjoy a lifetime of fulfillment and happiness. Their bond will become one of love and respect and will meet the expectations of our Sages: "He [the husband] is to love her as his own self and to respect her even more than his own self, and she [the wife] is to respect her husband to the utmost extreme" (Rambam, *Hilchos Ishus* 15:19-20). This approach, based on the nature and needs of man and woman, will lead to a life of love and devotion.

This complementary relationship between husband and wife may be likened to the right and left hands of one body. Their roles may differ, but they are complementary, and the more each respects the other's role, the more effectively the two hands will function together.

Men and women were created with obvious anatomical and physiologic differences, as well as psychological and emotional differences. In fact, recent scientific discoveries have come to the conclusion that these gender differences have to do with the biology of the brain. "Cognitive variations between the sexes reflect differing hormonal influences on brain development. Thus, men and women differ not only in physical attributes and reproductive function, but also in the way in which they solve intellectual problems" (*Scientific American*, September 1992).

In fact, we know that their differences extend even to the spiritual dimension. Women are exempt from positive mitzvos which are time-bound. And we know that mitzvos are given to us to help us improve ourselves. Therefore, women are exempt from certain mitzvos because they do not need them. A woman is exempt from these commandments, not because she is lacking in any way, but because she is *not* lacking in those ways. To fulfill her spiritual potential, she does not need those particular mitzvos.

Why, in fact, did G-d create her in such a way that she would not be bound to these particular commandments? The reason given by our Sages (*Kolbo* 23) is that if the woman had been bound to listen to G-d and this would conflict with her husband's needs, it would create a conflict in her. So G-d exempted her from these mitzvos, due to her important role as wife.

One of our great Sages expressed this clear recognition of his wife's importance to him: "I never called my wife 'my wife,' but rather, 'my home'" (*Gittin* 52a). The woman is the essence of the home; it is her sphere of responsibility. But as in all of life, we walk along a very narrow bridge, and we need to always be balancing between appreciating our vital position and not flaunting superiority to our husbands because of this responsibility.

*   *   *

A parable is told by the Chofetz Chaim about a man who arrived at an inn one night, looking for lodgings. Due to the fact that an army regiment was staying there, all the rooms were taken. Trying to help the man out, the innkeeper agreed to allow him the use of one of the rooms until the early morning. This room was occupied by the general in command, who was out for the night. The only condition the innkeeper made with the man was that he vacate the room by the time the general came in the morning. The man accepted the offer thankfully, requesting that the innkeeper wake him up at the crack of dawn. Then the weary traveler put on his nightshirt, climbed into bed and fell fast asleep.

It was still quite dark when the innkeeper woke him up. "Hurry! Hurry! The general is coming!" he called. Still half-asleep, the traveler dressed hurriedly, but without realizing, he put on the general's clothes instead of his own. Gathering his belongings, he began making his way to his horse and cart. But as he was leaving the inn, he happened

to glance at a full-length mirror that decorated the front
door.

"Dear me," he exclaimed, "what a silly mistake the
innkeeper made. He woke the general instead of me!"

*   *   *

Even though a woman often finds herself in a position
of authority, she must realize that her inwardly directed,
womanly nature does not change. If she imagines she is
something or someone she is not, she will contradict her
own essence and suffer the consequences.

For a marital relationship to thrive, we have to understand and appreciate our different natures and responsibilities. A man's nature is outwardly directed, and a woman's
nature is inwardly directed. Because there is more recognition given to external achievements in Western culture,
we've come to see publicly recognized activities as the
most desirable. We've come to easily accept these values,
though, without even seeing proof that public acclaim leads
to greater happiness, fulfillment or peace of mind.

Neither nature is superior. The outwardly and inwardly directed natures are complementary, each enhancing the other. Recognizing these differences and
understanding our distinct roles is crucial to a successful
marriage. It can literally make or break a marriage.

*   *   *

"Mrs. Cohen!" Abby cried out when she bumped into
the woman with whom she had studied prior to her
marriage, three months earlier. "I just have to thank you for
giving me such a clear explanation about role differences
in marriage." "Let me tell you," she continued, "I would have

been divorced by now had I not gotten that concept straight before my wedding!"

Mrs. Cohen simply smiled, remembering well Abby's initial negative reaction during their discussions. She was delighted that the time spent confronting this basic issue with Abby had certainly not been in vain.

*   *   *

It is never too late, though, to understand this important concept and put it into practice. Recognition of our many gender differences is needed for a happy, functioning marriage. Until a woman is at ease with her essence and sphere of responsibilities, not only will she be fighting often with her husband, but she will be in a constant, stressful battle with herself, going through the motions, feeling like a martyr and all the time experiencing tremendous tension. It is not conducive to peace with her husband, or her own inner peace, to carry on day after day like that. So we have to come to terms with who we really are and what our essence really is.

A husband and wife need to respect each other's spheres of responsibility. Confusion about these responsibilities is very dangerous, and the result of this confusion is evident in the tremendous rise in the divorce rate in recent years. The reason why present-day lives are so stressful is that, in a wide variety of ways, we are trying to go against nature.

The Torah guidelines are clearly laid out for us, exactly suited to our innate natures. The natural tendency of the woman is to desire her husband's sheltering and assuring role in marriage (see *Bereshis* 3:16). And the natural tendency of the man is to desire to be in the sheltering and assuring role in marriage (ibid.). Recognizing the natural tendencies with which distinct kinds of human beings were endowed is the basis for creating a harmonious relationship between them. In short, every man wants to be "the man" in his home, and every woman wants him to be the man in the home.

*   *   *

A local villager had married a domineering woman with a fierce temper. Often, in the heat of an argument, the poor man would meekly crouch under the table. He would wait for his wife to calm down, unwilling to engage in continuous bickering. The woman would eventually relax and order her husband out from under the table. Obediently, he would emerge only to retreat again at the next sign of a blowup.

A neighbor happened to come by in the midst of one of these episodes. The scene he witnessed was beyond his comprehension. He bent down to the husband, who sat crouched beneath the table.

"How can you let your wife do this to you? You must show her who is the real boss around the house!"

The neighbor's words impressed the husband. The next time his wife threw a fit, he quickly fled under the table as always. But then, he remembered his neighbor's words and decided to act on his advice. When his wife calmed down and beckoned him out from beneath the table, he adamantly refused to budge.

"I'm not going to listen to you this time," he retorted. "For once, I'll show you who is the boss!"

His newly acquired superiority and positive self-image gave him a very honored position — under the table.

*   *   *

It is important to know what a husband's natural character traits are, because if a woman tries very hard to break them, and she finally meets with "success," with whom will she be left? Either with a man who has only his masculine physical attributes left and is spiritually and psychologically unhealthy, or with no man at all in the home with her.

When a woman does not recognize her essence, she may end up nagging her husband to the point where he loses all conception of what it is to be a man. And who wants to remain married to a conquered man? So much pleasure has been drained out. A woman certainly has the ability to act superior to her husband, but will she then enjoy living with the man she has diminished?

It isn't helpful to show off feelings of superiority to a husband — not in public, and even not in private. A man is longing for a loyal, loving wife, not a teacher. The wife's challenge is to show him respect, even at times when it is difficult for her. She has to try her best to accept her husband as he is. If there is something she feels she has to correct in him, the only way to try that could possibly be genuinely successful, is gently, lightly and with warmth, never from a point of superiority. This applies even when issues are of a religious nature.

*   *   *

Suri was going to a series of classes on the laws of *lashon hara*, which deal with refraining from speaking negatively about people. She felt that she was quite an expert on the subject, and she found every opportunity to show off her "expertise" on her poor husband. He was frequently told in private, and in public, to "Stop speaking *lashon hara!*"

*   *   *

There are ways to handle these situations without compromising the husband-wife relationship. Putting him down is not one of them, though.

*   *   *

Tova's husband saw a pile of dirty dishes in the sink after his wife had gone to bed, and he washed them up. When Tova got up in the morning and saw the dishes done, she didn't bother to thank her husband for doing them. "Why should I?" she reasoned to herself. "Why should I make him feel like he did me such a big favor? I was exhausted. He should do the dishes *more* often. He uses more of them than I do anyway."

*   *   *

There is no rule that says a husband can't wash dishes, or change diapers, or cook meals. But it must be remembered that he is *helping her* with *her* sphere of responsibility. Tova was mistaken. The dishes *are* her responsibility. He *was* helping her. And appreciation is the basis of an open, loving communication. She should thank him for whatever he does, even if he's doing it on a regular basis. She should thank him for helping with her domain, but she should also not forget to thank him for what he does for her in his sphere of responsibility too.

Just because responsibilities are being defined, this does not at all cut out teamwork and cooperation. The opposite occurs. When positions are clear, a team can function more efficiently and harmoniously. A husband and wife share a life together. When we need help, we should say so as pleasantly as we can, in a straightforward manner. We can offer to help our husbands with their responsibilities too, remaining clear, though, that neither domain is superior to the other. We may have been repeatedly brainwashed throughout our lives to believe that "a woman's work is what a man doesn't want to do." But the sooner we recognize how that "grass is always greener on the other side" attitude has made women unnecessarily discontent for years, the sooner we can stop missing out on the profound pleasure available only to women in tune with their inner-directed essence.

We are not advocating an attitude wherein the most sparkling floor and perfect seven-layer cake are the highest goals toward which to strive. That limited type of existence is exactly what caused some women, understandably, to want to race out of their homes, craving fulfillment. What we are advocating is a return to our deepest selves and our most meaningful goals. These can be obtained within our homes, without the need to "to race out."

Sometimes, though, the roles may be reversed temporarily. For example, the husband may be studying, and the wife may be working outside of the home. But there has to be an effort put into remembering that she is only helping him with his sphere of responsibility — to support the family. She has not taken over the responsibility.

*   *   *

"What's this?!" Aviva asked her husband, who was holding a new pair of men's shoes in his hand. "*I'm* the one earning most of the money! You can't just go out and buy a new pair of shoes for yourself. Please return them tomorrow, if you don't mind. We simply can't afford them this month. I'm very sorry."

*   *   *

She isn't nearly as sorry as she will be later, if her domineering behavior continues much longer.

Money is a subject often fought about between many couples. First and foremost, we need to know that every Rosh HaShanah it is decreed exactly how much of it a person will have for the upcoming year. So, if a husband spends foolishly, it won't help for a wife to tell him off. She'll never really get through to him that way, anyway. It will cause a negative reaction instantaneously: he will quickly put up his defenses and try to justify himself. So many conflicts are a result of those little green paper things.

In case of a shortage of money, a woman should not blame her husband. Instead, she needs to be supportive, remembering that they are not really two separate beings. Deep down, they are one. The right hand and the left hand don't fight with each other; they support and help each other out. If she has any helpful suggestions, she should make them lovingly, and not act high and mighty about any area in which she is better than him. If, for instance, she is more adept at managing money than he is, she should check herself periodically to be sure that she is not acting superior to him.

And if *she* is the one spending money foolishly, she should apologize when he is upset with her. A man is not like a woman, who, when upset with someone, has a hard time getting over the painful feelings that become a part of her very deeply and quickly. Though it may be much more vehement, a man's anger is usually external only, and he does not ordinarily harbor truly hateful feelings nearly as readily. By apologizing, it is therefore surprisingly easy to calm a man down, and he will generally not hesitate to forget the whole argument right then and there.

But back to the spending problem, feeling a need for all kinds of things is an attempt to escape reality. Everything is lacking in a woman's life when she is lacking love and inner calmness. Trying to run away from facing these lacks in her life makes her more and more nervous and tense. Instead, the woman needs to admit to them and face them, and then she can work on finally following the steps that will lead directly to satisfying her very real underlying needs.

Many of a woman's demands may be a result of trying to compete with her friends on her husband's account. Failure in this competition is a sure thing. It will always seem to her, no matter what she gets, that her friends are happier and more successful than she is, because they are not going to show her all their failures. On the other hand, her friends are sure that she is happier and more successful than they are! So why should she put unnecessary pressure on herself and drag her husband right down with her?

*　　　*　　　*

Nechama and her husband were in a fancy store, choosing a set of china. The choice had been narrowed down to two sets that looked very similar, but one was double the price of the other.

With an extremely worried look on his face, Raphael whispered to the storekeeper, "Please, say you are out of stock and unable to order the higher-priced one. I simply cannot afford it."

Nechama, not completely out of earshot as her husband had thought, overheard the whispering and realized for the very first time how insensitive she had been with her money spending. She resolved on the spot that from then on she would make every effort to share her husband's burden.

*   *   *

If a woman has a problem with spending too much money, or any other issue for that matter, she needs to first seek advice from her husband before turning to others for *their* suggestions. That is a wonderful policy to start implementing.

*   *   *

Batsheva was sitting with the rabbi's wife and analyzing her shaky marriage. She described all the things she did for her husband. "I make his favorite dishes, I entertain his guests, I iron his shirts and I always make myself look nice. I'm really such a good wife, but he never does anything I want him to do."

She gave herself away, though, when she gave a specific example of what she meant. "Take last night, for instance," she began. "I was serving meatloaf and potatoes for dinner, when my husband asked if he could have the leftover chicken and rice from Shabbos."

"So what did you do?" asked the rabbi's wife.

"I told him, 'Of course not! Why should you have to have something different from the children?!?' Do you know what confusion that creates for me? Then suddenly all the children would refuse to eat what I had made and they'd want what *he* wanted! Some nerve he has trying to make everything extra-hard for me all the time!"

Now it became clear what the problem was. Next came Batsheva's chance to learn how to treat her husband royally and begin to live with him as only a queen could live with a king.

*   *   *

A woman once came to the Ponivitzer Rav, crying bitterly about her husband's despicable behavior toward her. The Rav listened sympathetically. When his assistant, who had been present while she spoke, asked if he believed all those things the woman had been saying about her husband, the Rav said, "Certainly. Words spoken in truth are recognizable."

But the Rav's assistant was genuinely mystified. "How could this man, who had been known as a very decent fellow, lower himself to such behavior?" he begged to understand.

And so the Rav explained to him that when a man gets attacked at his most vulnerable point (his male ego) on a continuous basis, it can result in a tremendous deterioration in his behavior. This is a subconscious reaction to save himself from feeling as if all his power has been taken away from him. In these desperate attempts to defend his own honor, his logic can become totally crooked, until he, himself, will not understand how he could have possibly stooped so low.

"The answer," said the Ponivitzer Rav, "is for his wife to build him back up to the position of king in their home. This will prevent such situations from recurring, since then there will no longer be any reason for the husband to *demand* his own honor. A king can afford to be very kindhearted, as he feels assured of his esteemed position and does not live in fear of being put down."

*　　　*　　　*

The Midrash quotes one wise woman's advice to her daughter upon her marriage:

"My daughter, stand before your husband and treat him like a king. If you will serve him as a maidservant, he will return that service to you and honor you as his queen. However, if you try to dominate him, he will be master over you, and then he will consider you as a lowly maidservant" (*Menoras HaMaor*).

We are promised a reward in the World to Come for this appropriate way of behaving, and in this world too, our lives will take a dramatic change for the better when we try to treat our husbands as we would treat kings. It is wondrous to see. When a woman begins to revere her husband, while maintaining her own dignity completely, she almost immediately feels more feminine, and also noble. She suddenly has the makings of a queen.

What does it mean for a wife to "treat him like a king"? It means, for example, trying hard to please him, being enthusiastic about his ideas, being straightforward and stating her preferences, but accepting his final decision. It is amazing how well and how quickly it feels congruous, as we allow our natural selves to be expressed in this royal relationship.

If we forgo our wishes for his wishes and even give his wishes priority over our children's, it will be one of the greatest gifts we can give our children: proof of the endearment and respect that we have for their father. We need to make castles for our husbands. That means we clearly wouldn't shout at him for doing something like dirtying the floor. We're making a home for our husbands, so that they have a place in which to feel completely comfortable — a home to *live* in, not just to look at. A home needs naturalness.

We need to always be on the lookout for what makes him happy, in every aspect of living. And we must try to fulfill as many of those desires as we can. When he's sad, we should help him to feel better. When something painful happens to him, we should comfort him. We should honor his parents and his family. And if a husband gives even a little gift, we need to show him real appreciation for it. We should never push a husband away with coldness, or put him down in any way. Instead, we must build our husbands up.

Understanding the underlying principle will make it easy for us to adopt these Torah guidelines in our married lives. For we must understand that there are some men who have a strong desire to be in charge of other people, and there are others who have very little desire to do that. A man who has little desire to direct others will prefer a job in which he takes orders from other people, rather than give orders to others. But the fact is, in his home, even *this* kind of man, who has hardly any desire to direct others, will, because of his masculine nature, still desire to be ruler. This is the nature of his being.

It is simply natural for every man to be the ruler in his home. If every woman would accept and stop fighting this fact, there would be so many more peaceful homes, as this is one of the most basic foundations upon which a home stands. A woman needs to be extremely careful not to hurt, even by mistake, her husband's genuinely fragile male ego.

Any woman who tries to ignore her husband's need to govern his home — and thereby goes against human nature — will end up greatly harming both her husband and herself. She will inadvertently ruin her family with her own hands. An unwillingness to accept this reality has caused an untold number of marriages to break up, and even when the marriages do stay together, there is a constant undercurrent of tension and unhappiness in the home.

There will be so many big and little issues that cause a giant question mark to appear before her eyes. "Doesn't he realize how much more insightful and astute I am in these kinds of situations?" "With *all his faults*, I'm supposed to respect everything he says?" "With all these hard-earned degrees after my name, I still need to 'bow my head' to my husband as if I haven't got any will of my own?" "My opinion isn't worth as much as his?" "Don't I have my own needs, my own wants, my own thoughts?" Is the woman going to be able to give in to her husband's wishes when questions like that often plague her? Is she going to be willing to defer to his opinion? Not too often. Instead come the endless arguments that, if the couple remain together, are still going on even after their grandchildren have gotten married.

On the other hand, a woman who "succeeds" in controlling her husband, until he is the one who is always forgoing and always listening to everything she says, will be left with a frustrated husband who lacks confidence and who is looked down upon by others, by her and by himself. She doesn't have to be a genius to be able to dominate her husband. She just has to know a few things about him. She has to be able to pick up on all his weak points, know exactly how to talk, when to talk, how to persuade him, when to turn the pressure up and then when to get all tearful. She has to remain determined to manipulate him until he gives in totally and does exactly what she wants him to do.

Whether the woman uses verbal badgering or tearful "water power" to win her way, someone whose wife rules him becomes a half-man. Even if she irons his shirts, bakes cakes for him, prepares his food and talks to him as sweetly as can be, she may still be ruling over her husband and keeping him on a leash, just more discreetly than an obviously bossy wife.

We're talking about something much deeper than what one sees outwardly. This is an idea of tremendous depth. When a man gets hurt repeatedly at his most sensitive points, a situation is created in which the individual is constantly on the defensive, and in his subconscious, he is always struggling for control. He may become very stubborn and overly sensitive about picky, little things. He becomes a frustrated little man, desperate to win any tiny battle he can, to "prove" himself still a capable leader.

The constant inner tension which "dethroned" men like that live with has long-term repercussions. The man himself does not have the insight to see what is happening, and he is likely to keep sliding downward. People wonder, "What happened to this man? He used to be bright, honest and clear-thinking." He turns obstinate, suspicious of people and illogical, with an enormous inferiority complex.

An obvious reason, therefore, why it is a good idea for a woman to make her husband into a king is because a king is more likely to have a good heart. The smaller a man feels he is, the more he needs to prove his strength and importance at any opportunity that comes his way. A low-level clerk in a government office will be harsher, more bureaucratic and more picky than the executive we'd deal with if we went straight to the top. The top management will usually be able to be more open-hearted, and with them we could work out a feasible plan, because they are not afraid of losing their status if they defer to our wishes. Their self-esteem is not so shaky.

If the individuals in the marital unit are not complementing one another correctly, they will suffer in their other human relations as well. Since life is like going up a ramp, if we aren't making a big effort to climb constantly, we will go down. There's no staying in one place. A wife can, through all her warm ways, be constantly encouraging her husband to grow. If she makes him feel like he's wonderful, he will *become* wonderful! The wife could also be the one, however, to constantly push her husband down further and further every day.

We all know men who seemed to be potentially great achievers before they got married, but whose growth was stunted as time went on. On the other hand, we know men who were mediocre when single, but who suddenly started progressing after marriage and developed tremendously, way beyond ordinary understanding. We may cringe at first, but please G-d, someday we'll be grinning, fully recognizing the validity and value of the old saying, "Behind every great man, there is a great woman."

We will be better able to focus on our husbands' good qualities, and to come to admire and eventually revere him, if we begin by focusing on our own good qualities. Taking pleasure in ourselves is a prerequisite to taking pleasure in others. Being kind both to ourselves and to others powerfully increases the positive feelings that we have about ourselves.

We may begin doing something kind for our husbands with a grouchy and sour face because, although we know we should, we really don't feel like it. But the action itself can create good feelings in us very soon, if we allow it to. We just need to keep in mind these two Torah principles: 1) The heart follows the action, and 2) A person is helped (by heaven) along the way he wants to go.

Our Sages have taught us that every blade of grass has a *malach* (an angel) appointed over it, to make it grow. The wife is like that angel. She is appointed over her husband to make him grow into a king. Then she will have reason to enjoy a double celebration — for his coronation as king and for her coronation as his beloved queen.

*   *   *

Rachel could have married the most pious, scholarly and wealthiest man of her choice. But she chooses, for reasons known only to herself, a forty-year-old shepherd who not only is penniless, but also has never learned a word of Torah in his life.

Despite her family's objection, she marries the shepherd, Akiva. The only condition she makes with him is that he will go and learn Torah after they are married. However, after the wedding, Akiva refuses to go to the house of study to learn Torah. He is very embarrassed that he will be laughed at there because of his ignorance.

Rachel understands his feelings, and she realizes that nagging will not work. She devotes her intellectual powers to the problem, uses her creative talents and figures out the best thing to try in order to correct the situation, while retaining peace in her home.

Rachel searches the marketplace until she finds, after much effort, exactly what she is looking for — a donkey with two humps on its back, like a camel, an unusual species. She then puts soil between the two humps and plants some vegetables there. The following day she sets out with Akiva and the donkey to the marketplace. There they station the donkey at the entrance and step back to watch what would happen.

The whole first day, their donkey is a great attraction. People crowd around to stare at this funny-looking creature. But as the days go by, they just get used to him being there. Fewer and fewer people take any notice of him.

Rachel smiles up at her husband and says very gently, "Go and learn Torah, Akiva. Don't worry about the people laughing at you. How long will their laughter last? One or two days at the most. They will surely learn that there is Akiva, the *am ha'aretz*, the one who doesn't yet know Torah, and that there is also Akiva, the *talmid chacham*, the scholar."

Akiva heeds his wife's encouraging words, and he sets out on his way to study Torah. When he returns as the famous Rabbi Akiva with his twenty-four thousand students behind him, he makes way for his wife, who is in the huge crowd to welcome him. Then he declares before his students, for all to hear and know these illuminating words forever: "*All that I have* — and all that you have — all belongs to her!" (Midrash)

*   *   *

When our husbands return from synagogue on Friday night, they are escorted by two malachim (angels) who ask three questions, all directed to the queen of the home:

"Shulchan aruch? — Is the table set?"

"*Mita mutzas?* — Is the bed made?"

"*Ner doleik?* — Is the candle lit?"

These three questions pertain to the three mitzvos

which were given specifically to women.

The first: "Is the table set?" refers to the taking of dough, which, in fact, is symbolic of all the acts of *chesed* (kindness), with which we, as women, fill our homes.

The second: "Is the bed made?" refers to the mitzvah of *taharas hamishpachah* (family purity), which, in fact, is symbolic of the *taharah* (purity) of the home, which we, as wives, were granted the key to safeguard and bring into our marriages.

The third: "Is the candle lit?" refers to the mitzvah of *hadlakas haner* (candlelighting), which, in fact, is symbolic of the *shalom* (peace) in our home, the light which is ours to ignite.

May these two *malachim* forever be answered in the affirmative by a queen in every Jewish home, so that once again it will be "in the merit of righteous women" that our nation shall emerge from *galus* (exile). Then may we all merit to see the coming of Mashiach, who will arrive, our Sages teach us, with the greeting of…"Shalom!"

Book Two:

From Man to Man:
On Being a Husband

Introduction

The institution of marriage is under siege. In the Western culture, divorce rates hover around an unparalleled fifty percent.

Due to pressures of the nineties and extraordinary social confusion, levels of discord in marriage are at an all-time high.

To meet this challenge, an enormous industry of researchers, analysts and counselors has sprung up. "How to Save Your Marriage" manuals constantly top the bestseller charts.

The Jewish people, dispersed among the nations, and all too often overintegrated, have also been affected by these phenomena. Many of them have recourse to non-Jewish sources for guidance, direction and counseling in their marriages.

*   *   *

The story is told of a Russian nobleman who wished to experience rail travel for the first time. Dressed in his best, he comes to purchase a ticket. The clerk recognizes a nobleman and naturally issues him a first-class ticket. Being a novice to rail travel, the nobleman blunders into the first coach he encounters, which happens to be third class. He is somewhat dismayed at the primitive furnishings, and his fellow travelers are rowdy passengers.

With the train well on its way, the nobleman notices the peasants producing their tickets in anticipation of the conductor's inspection. He cannot understand why all their tickets are blue while his is red. He asks his neighbor the peasant for an explanation. Seeing that he is a novice, the peasant decides to have some fun with this naive nobleman.

Enlisting his fellow peasants to the cause, the peasant and his comrades all caution him that he has not paid enough and those ruthless conductors will immediately evict him from the train. The nobleman gratefully complies when one of them suggests he hide under the bench. As the conductor is about to leave, one of the peasants points out to him the stowaway. After hauling him out, the conductor begins to berate him until the nobleman apologetically produces his first-class ticket. The conductor, realizing what has happened, says, "Foolish man, you could have been traveling first class in comfort. However, since you didn't bother to find out about rail travel, you are not only traveling third class, but third class under the bench!"

*   *   *

Too many Jews, unaware that Torah has a timeless formula for marriage, avail themselves of the non-Jewish system. This system, floundering in its own confusion and responding to a promiscuous culture, has nothing to offer the Jew.

The objective of this book is to present the intimate elements of the Jewish marriage from a Torah perspective.

Very little concentrated literature exists on these matters, for the simple reason that, while this once was an art passed down from father to son, in the confusion of our times the art is being lost. Therefore, we humbly apply *"Eis la'asos Lashem* — There is a time to do for G-d."

It is our prayer that every Jew should merit a proper education in these matters and build a *bayis ne'eman b'Yisrael* — a true Jewish home.

ONE

Striving for Excellence

The charismatic tzaddik (pious man) of Jerusalem, R. Aryeh Levin, *ztz"l*, once accompanied his wife to the doctor. When the doctor asked the couple what was the matter, R. Aryeh answered, "My wife's foot hurts us." R. Aryeh felt the pain of his wife's foot. This charming anecdote sums up for us what we are striving for in a marriage. Our goal is *v'hayu l'vasar echad*, to fulfill G-d's command to Adam that man and wife should be as one flesh (*Bereshis* 2:24). They should realize a complete merging of personalities, desires and feelings.

Rabbi Aharon Kotler, *ztz"l*, the Rosh Yeshivah and founder of the Lakewood Yeshivah, had a direct tradition from the Vilna Gaon, *ztz"l*, that the purpose of marriage is to create *hisachdus beineihem v'ribbui ahavah*, a unity between them and a bounty of love (*Mishkan Yisrael*).

The *Sefer HaChinuch* gives us an insight into the mitzvah of *m'sameach ishto b'shanah rishonah*, of giving happiness to one's wife in the first year of marriage. He says the purpose of the mitzvah is *k'dei l'hargil hateva imah u'l'hadbik haratzon etzlah*, to align one's personality and nature with his wife's and to forge together their desires and goals. We see that this is not a relationship in which we should simply learn how to coexist. The Torah's expectations of marriage are very high.

There is a story told about R. Shlomo Zalman Auerbach, *shlita*, Rosh Yeshivah of Yeshivas Kol Torah, which proves that, even today, it is possible to meet these high standards. There is a custom at funerals in Jerusalem that, at the time of burial, the relatives of the departed stand before the casket and ask for forgiveness. At his wife's funeral, as he stood at the open grave site, R. Shlomo Zalman was heard to say that in all his years of marriage, he could not recall a single instance where he caused his wife pain. He couldn't think of anything for which he needed to apologize (*The River, the Kettle, and the Bird*). We see that even in our generation, replete with marital strife, we are capable of perfectly harmonious marriages.

To properly understand the intricate relationship of a marriage, we must note a unique distinction between this relationship and all other familial relationships. The relationship between spouses is not innate. It is not a natural, inherent, blood relationship, and it is this distinction which creates an inherent fragility in the structure of marriage. The fact that there is an escape clause (divorce) underscores this vulnerability. A marriage is the coming together of two individuals with different backgrounds, personalities and genetic makeups. They are different in terms of mannerisms and inclinations, and this can be a highly disruptive factor.

Other familial relationships do not have this weakness. The innate blood relationship that exists between parents and children, brothers and sisters, and even grandparents and grandchildren is an inherently stronger relationship. In these blood relationships, strong bonds are formed from the beginning of the relationship. These bonds help to implant deep feelings of love and devotion which enable the relationships to withstand tremendous tension and insult. The threshold of tolerance is almost limitless. This is not the case in a marriage.

In a marriage, the husband and wife first meet each other with their personalities already formed. They are now expected to integrate these two distinct personalities, with all of their idiosyncrasies, into one happy unit. This can make for a volatile situation. A certain level of belligerence which would be tolerated by another member of the family can easily bring about a situation of hatred in a marriage. There are times when siblings have major clashes, and parents sometimes take outrageous abuse from their children (and vice versa), yet these relationships survive. This same level of discord in a marriage will often lead to divorce. On the other hand, this is the only relationship in which such extraordinary heights of intimacy and closeness are achievable. It is this same relationship which can be either a source of intense hostility or a *binyan adei ad*, a building for eternity.

This is what the Gemara is referring to when it tells us, "*Ish v'ishah: zachu, Shechinah beineihem; lo zachu, eish achalan*" (*Sotah* 17a). If a man and a woman are meritorious, the Divine Presence is between them; if they are not meritorious, fire consumes them. This completely unique relationship is capable of being either a vehicle of harmony upon which the Divine Presence can rest, or it can be a union which is destroyed by a fire of discord.

Because a marriage can swing to such extremes, it requires a continual input and a commitment which is constantly renewed. Of course, none of our relationships should be taken for granted, but a marriage will likely not continue to exist if it is taken for granted. Unfortunately, many do not make this distinction, but they treat their marriage like any other relationship. Instead, they make an incorrect assumption that the success of their marriage is guaranteed. "After all," they reason, "we love each other." What happens is that when faced with the myriad issues which confront a young couple, working on the relationship is often relegated to the lowest of priorities. The truth, though, is that a successful marriage needs continual work, especially in the beginning.

This is why the Torah mandates special laws regarding *shanah rishonah*, the first year of marriage. This first year is a time when tremendous care and energy are expended to establish as close a relationship as possible. It is the period in the young couple's lives to set the tone for trust, commitment and caring. These are ingredients which are essential for the future years to establish the dwelling of the Shechinah between them, and to protect them from being consumed by fire. This *shanah rishonah* is, of course, only a model for their whole life together.

*   *   *

This is not to suggest that the *shanah rishonah* is an all-or-nothing opportunity. Naturally, any situation is salvageable at any stage, as is illustrated by a story told of Reb Yisrael Salanter. It was the end of the day, and Reb Yisrael needed his shoe mended. He took the shoe to a cobbler and asked him if there was still time left in the day to fix it. The cobbler glanced at his waning candle and responded, "All the while that the candle burns, I can work."

Reb Yisrael, delighted with this statement, repeated it to himself several times, realizing how appropriately it could be applied to all of life's challenges. As long as the candle is burning, as long as we are involved in a situation, we can work. This is certainly the case with marriage. At any stage, a couple can remedy a situation and start afresh.

TWO

Fragility in Marriage

After G-d created the world, there was still one missing component. In order for the world to be complete, there was one creature which still needed to be brought into existence. For the creation to be perfect, there had to be a woman.

Hashem declares, *"Lo tov heyos ha'adam levado, e'eseh lo aizer k'negdo* — It is not good for the man to be alone; I will make him a helpmate opposing him" (*Bereishis* 2:18). We see in this very first mention of the husband-wife relationship that there is an element of contrariness. This same woman who is created as a helpmate is also *k'negdo*; she is an opposing force. The Torah is telling us very clearly that a man and a woman, by their natures, are set against each other. Nevertheless, every Jewish man is commanded to find his own contrary helpmate and to get married.

With this in mind, if we are to objectively analyze the chances of a marriage being successful, a dismal picture arises. Instead of a fairy-tale romance of living happily ever after, we see that this *k'negdo* element is multi-faceted.

Physiologically, psychologically and emotionally, men and women are vastly different. It is hard to imagine how they could possibly live together without tremendous discord.

Further, by the time a bride and groom come to the *chuppah*, the wedding canopy, their personalities are formed. Each one has had completely unique life experiences. The differences in their upbringings have etched out character traits, habits and attitudes which have become an integral part of their personalities. Our Sages have likened these formative experiences, the *girsa d'yankusa*, as indelible ink written onto a clean slate. With the inherent gender-related dissimilarities and the two distinctive personalities involved in a marriage, it seems unreasonable to expect two young newlyweds to share every aspect of their lives together without conflict.

*   *   *

A young man came to his rabbi a few weeks after his wedding. This man was visibly bothered and he needed little prodding to open up. "Rabbi, I'm embarrassed to admit that there is already tension in our marriage. But I'm even more embarrassed to tell you what the issue is." Mustering up his courage, he finally confessed, "You see, I roll, and she squeezes."

Despite his wisdom, the rabbi had no idea what was being rolled and squeezed. Before he asked for clarification, the young groom continued. "I've tried telling her several times that it's cleaner and much more efficient to nicely roll the tube of toothpaste, but she insists on grabbing the tube and squeezing it with her whole hand. She says that this is how she's always done it, and that she simply can't be bothered to change." The young man was overwhelmed by the brilliance of the rabbi's advice to buy two tubes of toothpaste.

*   *   *

This ridiculous (yet common) example illustrates that there can be significant differences on almost every level of a relationship. Whether it is the selection of the furniture and decor, the discovery of culinary preferences and practices, the saving and spending habits, the attitudes towards in-laws, or the social practices of who, how and when to entertain, the issues are nearly endless. Once childrearing enters into the picture, with its whole new range of issues, an already rocky relationship will now become explosive. So too, at every new junction in life, there is potential discord which can surface.

People are often deeply committed and emotionally attached to the way that they were (or were not) raised. Each person is convinced that his system is the only one. A person relies on the argument of "It worked for me!" or "I turned out all right, didn't I?!" Our parents are our ultimate role models. We spend our entire formative years observing our own families. Behavior patterns and attitudes become entrenched in our minds (often very subtly), and we come into marriage with a very firm idea of the right way.

There have been countless hours of marriage counseling meted out because people take unshakable stands over trivialities. Objectively, it seems absurd that a husband shouldn't bring his wife a drink in the morning if it will make her happy. After all, she grew up in a home where her father always brought her mother a cup of water in the morning. Yet he insists upon taking an unshakable stand because he grew up in a home where he never saw his father bring drinks to his mother. Similarly, a man who never saw his father washing dishes is shocked at his wife's expectation that he participate in domestic chores. We mirror what we have seen at home, and we adopt the view that it is unthinkable to do otherwise.

Conversely, some people subconsciously resolve never to repeat certain patterns which they see at home. This, too, can lead to stubborn stands and decisions which are not based on logic.

There are two additional factors challenging a marriage which are unique to our generation. They are the women's liberation movement and the mass media. The women's liberation movement was one of the most powerful social revolutions in history. Over a period of approximately twenty years, the attitudes of an entire generation throughout the world were challenged and changed. This massive upheaval of traditional values and overturning of the delineation of gender roles has taken its toll on nearly every level of society, and it has contributed greatly to adding confusion to the husband-wife relationship.

The second factor which adds further challenges to a marriage is the media. We are living in a time when it is practically impossible to escape from the atmosphere of the media. Advertising is a multi-billion dollar industry whose sole aim is to constantly beam messages into our minds. Our senses are continually being assailed as we drive or walk through any non-residential neighborhood. Like the dripping of water onto a rock, the media subtly plants ideas into our hearts, souls and minds. Unfortunately, the institution which is communicating these messages is part of a society which has a horrendous failure rate in marital harmony.

For the last two thousand years, Jews have lived in

a tremendous array of societies, yet we have always been able to keep our identity. Despite being surrounded by constantly changing social winds, we were able to stay devoutly committed to our values. Our homes functioned as a *mishkan me'at,* a miniature sanctuary, to protect our families from the sometimes brutal outside world. But today, our *mishkan me'at* is threatened.

With the sophistication and widespread availability of every form of media, all our senses are under attack. Televisions, radios, billboards, newspapers and magazines are all replete with messages (sometimes subtle, sometimes glaring) which are not at all in line with the values and morals of a Jew. It is nearly impossible for anyone to live a normal life without being affected by this inundation from the media. These messages slowly creep into our minds, and they subconsciously affect us, especially in our formative years. We can no longer assume that a *chasan* and *kallah* will approach their wedding day with the precious inno-cence which in the past was taken for granted. They often stand beneath the *chuppah* with minds which are partially cluttered with foreign images and influences. These are often bound up with unhealthy attitudes and expectations which put strains on a marriage.

Too frequently, a young couple finds serious discord tearing apart their relationship. Desperately, one or both of them approaches a friend, rabbi or marriage counselor. They don't understand. The dating, engagement and wed-ding were dreamlike, but now they clash several times each day. And when they aren't quarreling, they are usually on edge so as not to start the next fight. This couple was sure that their "Once upon a time" beginning would culminate with a "They lived happily ever after" ending. Instead, they are tasting life's realities and difficulties.

It seems that the odds are heavily stacked against a serene and harmonious relationship between a husband and wife. However, shortly after mentioning the *aizer k'negdo*, the contrariness, the Torah goes on to describe the attainable goal, *"v'davak b'ishto v'hayu l'vasar echad — that a man should cling to his wife, and they should be one flesh"* (*Bereshis* 2:24).

THREE

Total Commitment

The cow and the chicken were walking down the road together, when the chicken noticed a billboard with an advertisement for a breakfast diner. The text of the billboard read, "We serve steak and eggs."

Excited, the chicken said to the cow, "Look, we're both famous; we made it together onto the billboard!"

The cow gruffly responded, "Don't compare the two of us. For you, it's a measly donation. For me, it's a total commitment."

*   *   *

In order to have a successful marriage, we have to totally commit ourselves. We need to learn to give of ourselves in every way. Perfunctory donations and token gestures are simply insufficient to face the plethora of challenges which a normal marriage brings. One necessary element in learning how to give with such totality is to view our marriages as an absolute — our wives as eternal partners.

Too frequently, a marriage goes through a strenuous time, and either the husband or the wife begins to have doubts concerning their spouse. "I could have done better." "I should have married so-and-so." People feel that they were deceived by their spouse and by the *shadchan* (matchmaker). They think, "I should have been told about such a glaring weakness!" This overreadiness to hopelessly throw up one's hands seems to have two sources of blame. The first is the era in which we live. This is a plastic generation, and because so much of the things in our lives are disposable, this influences the way we see the world. As a result, we also see relationships, even marriage, as disposable.

The second reason we are likely to give up on our marriages too quickly is because we lack appreciation that our marriage is a product of the Divine Matchmaker. We get so caught up in dating, engagements and wedding plans that we start to think that *we* are making this marriage. We forget that marriages are truly made in heaven. When two Jews are standing under the *chuppah*, this is divinely predestined. The Gemara says that forty days before conception, a heavenly voice declares, *"bas Ploni l'Ploni —* This person is destined for this person" (*Sotah* 2a). When we get married, we have found our soulmate. Although at times it may seem impossible, it is with this person that we are capable of achieving our potential. After the *chuppah*, there should never be an element of doubt.

The Chazon Ish says that the greatest joy a person can experience is the resolution of doubt. Perhaps this is one of the deeper reasons why there is such great joy at a wedding. For on the day of a man's wedding, there is a great resolution of doubt. Standing under the *chuppah*, the great question of "Who is my soulmate?" is resolved. A man must relate to his wife with a definitive attitude of, "You are my soulmate." A man must see his wife as if she is the only woman in the world.

This is eloquently expressed in one of the blessings said under the *chuppah.* We say in the fifth *berachah,* "*...k'samechachah yitzirchah b'Gan Eden mikedem —* ...just as You bestowed gladness on Your creation in the Garden of Eden from aforetime." The *simchah* that one feels at the finding of his soulmate should parallel the *simchah* that Adam HaRishon, the first man, felt at his wedding. What is this parallel? We should be as sure as Adam HaRishon was that we are marrying the right woman. Just as Adam HaRishon married the only woman in the world, a man should see himself as if he is marrying the only woman in the world.

Notwithstanding, there is the option of divorce. When a husband and wife are having a fight, there can be a temptation to bring up divorce as a means of settling everything. This is a terrible mistake, for it brings into question the permanence of the relationship. Divorce must be viewed only as an absolutely last resort. The fact that a husband and wife are soulmates means that they have the potential to work out their difficulties. They are capable of adjusting to each other's flaws and idiosyncrasies. This is only made possible, however, when there is an attitude of total and absolute commitment.

FOUR

The Inherent Difference

There is a very basic principle which has been viciously attacked in the last two decades — the simple idea that men and women are inherently different. As obvious as this may seem, the effects of the women's liberation movement on this idea have been awesome.

The women's movement had many valid claims. It was born as a result of women being abused by a male-dominated society, and their response was to strive for equality. Torah-observant Jews, however, have not had to respond to their claims, because our wives were never subjected to these abuses. They have never been relegated to secondary importance.

King David describes the woman as the *"akeres habayis"* (*Tehillim* 113:9). In modern Hebrew this would be translated as a housewife, but *"akeres"* is from the same root as *"ikar,"* essence. The woman is the essence of the home. The Jewish home is not a place of subordinate significance. This is the place where we attempt to erect our *mishkan me'at,* our miniature sanctuary. The woman is given the central role in creating this structure. If, however, she does not rise to this challenge, or if she is not elevated to this level of importance, she can become the *okeres habayis,* the uprooter of the house ("*okeres*" having the same root as "*akeres*" and "*ikar*").

The women's movement has had a tremendous impact, and elements of it have naturally spilled over to our Torah-observant society. This has caused us to question the basic teaching of the Torah that men and women are different. In the Torah, we see the differentiation between the sexes from the fact that there is a whole sector of *mitzvos* that women are not obligated to perform. Since *mitzvos* are given to refine and to purify our personalities, and women have fewer *mitzvos,* it means that there must be an inherent difference in the nature of men and women, and this difference extends to all dimensions.

This idea is expressed in the Hebrew words *panim* and *p'nim. Panim* (face) and *p'nim* (interior) have the exact same letters in the same order, because according to the Torah the *panim* is a reflection of the *p'nim.* No matter how hard this idea is attacked, it cannot be denied. Even if fashions and hairstyles and names all become unisex, it is plainly evident that there is an inherent physiological difference between men and women, and this difference in the *panim,* the external, is also a distinction to be found in the *p'nim,* the internal.

We also see that men and women are basically different when we look at the physiological patterns that men and women experience in their life cycles. Physically, men are basically stable. In a healthy male, from puberty until old age the only changes which take place in his body are those of a gradual aging process.

This is not the case with women. In a woman's body, from the day that she reaches puberty, her body begins a process of constant flux. There are continual huge changes taking place. Her monthly cycle dictates that every day her body is different from the day before. This cycle reaches a crescendo when the body is ready to become impregnated, and whether she becomes pregnant or not, her body again experiences a massive change. There are constantly tremendous hormonal changes taking place.

If a woman does become pregnant, the body begins gearing itself up for the incomparable trauma of childbirth. Her body experiences enormous changes throughout the pregnancy. Each day of the pregnancy, the actual birth, the postnatal stage and the time during lactation are all times of massive changes within a woman's body. The fluctuations are intense and continual. It is something that men can never truly fathom, yet we often act as if women should be able to approach life with the same attitudes that we have. This can be a tragic mistake. We are able to approach life with more emotional equilibrium because we have bodies which cater to such a disposition.

We simply cannot use our own feelings to try to understand our wives. This mistake of the husband using himself as a barometer for his wife's feelings is one of the greatest problems in *shalom bayis*. He can't understand why she stands on the table screaming just because she saw a cockroach. Why, he has no problem just swaggering over and crunching it beneath his masculine foot. Or perhaps he finds himself flapping around in a state of torment because he can't understand why today she's crying about the same thing that she laughed at yesterday. We must reanalyze the situation and realize that our wives have the right to these changes in disposition. Women have the right to pendular mood swings, to be weepy or bubbly for no apparent reason.

Men, however, have no such claim. Our bodies are relatively stable, and this provides, perhaps, one of the insights as to why certain obligations in the marriage are placed solely on the man. Under the *chuppah*, a man accepts upon himself the obligation of three *mitzvos* which the Torah refers to as "*sh'eir, k'sus, v'onah*" (see *Shemos* 21:10). The first two, *sh'eir* and *k'sus,* are relatively straightforward. They refer a man's obligation to provide his wife with food, clothing and shelter. It is the third obligation, the mitzvah of *onah,* which is often misunderstood. This mitzvah is often misconstrued to be referring solely to providing one's wife with her conjugal rights. Of course, *onah* does include the physical union, but it is a far more general mitzvah. The Steipler Gaon (*Iggeres HaKodesh*) writes that understanding and responding to her emotional needs and feelings is an integral part of this mitzvah.

There is, however, no corresponding mitzvah for the woman. Because we are physically more stable, we are the ones who are expected to create the atmosphere in the homes. We are the ones who need to be the anchor and stabilizing factor in this potentially tumultuous relationship.

The mitzvah of *onah* is entirely in the men's hands, and we have to view the success of the marriage to be largely on our shoulders. However, in order to properly fulfill this mitzvah and, in turn, to create *shalom bayis,* we must understand that there is this basic inherent difference between men and women. Without this understanding and the sensitivities which must accompany it, it is impossible to properly perform the mitzvah of *onah.*

FIVE

The Hedge of Roses

In a marriage guided by the Torah, the love between a man and a woman should steadily increase throughout their marriage. As they come to know each other better, they grow, meeting life's challenges together, sharing and giving to each other. This should be expressed in their intimate lives, where there also should be an ever-increasing love and respect, with the intimacy between them constantly growing in intensity. Although intimacy is not the exclusive basis of their love, they realize its central importance in bringing them closer and closer. As the Netziv writes, "Their intimacy shall bring them closer to becoming one" (*Ha'amek Davar, Bereshis* 2).

On the other hand, we see in the non-Torah world a growing concern with the boredom that sets in as the marriage progresses. This is loudly attested to by the high divorce rates, the hesitancy by many to get married and the preoccupation with the issue of marriages growing stale. Recent figures published by the British government show that the average duration of a marriage in 1990 in Western culture was nine-and-a-half years (Professor Richard White-field, chairman of the National Campaign for Family in Britain).

Some years ago, an area of research developed to attempt to better understand society's failure, as a whole, to succeed in marriage. This science sought to assess and analyze the intimate aspect of relationships. A school of thought emerged which pointed out that there is great difficulty in maintaining a healthy, wholesome and exciting intimate relationship. After many analyses, their conclusion was that in marriage there is an overfamiliarity which breeds contempt.

The Gemara (*Niddah* 31b), sensitive to this issue, explains that the underlying reason for the laws of *taharas mishpachah*, family purity, is that a man should not become overly familiar with his wife and therefore be repelled by her. Although this mitzvah of *taharas mishpachah* falls into the category of a *chok* — a mitzvah which defies human understanding and which we follow purely to observe G-d's will — our Sages offer us a glimpse into the reason for this mitzvah. And this reason is one which goes contrary to the thinking of many individuals.

People often make the mistake of focusing on the separation at the time when the woman is a *niddah*, and it can be viewed merely as a burden of self-control. It is clear from the Gemara, however, that one of the reasons for the separation is for the reunion. The Gemara says that the reason for the separation is that a woman should be as beloved by her husband on the night of her immersion in the *mikveh* as she was to him on their wedding night (*Niddah* 31b). It is clear that the Torah does not require this separation only for the sake of the separation. Rather, we separate so that at intervals the marriage is revitalized by the separation and the subsequent passionate reunion.

Inherent in the success of this system of disengagement and reunion is a strict adherence to a set of laws known as the *harchakos*, the limits instituted by our Sages which govern the physical relationship during the time that one's wife is a *niddah*. With their thorough and penetrating understanding of human nature, they established the *harchakos* to remove any strains of tension. The Sages forbade any activity which they felt could eventually lead to intimacy, and these *harchakos* must, therefore, be observed with meticulous care.

Included in these restrictions are any physical contact, the passing or throwing of objects and the sharing of food (*Shulchan Aruch, Yoreh De'ah* 195). These *harchakos* are referred to by the Gemara (*Sanhedrin* 37a) as a hedge of roses (*Shir HaShirim* 7:3). This hedge of roses serves as a protective border to prevent us from trespassing upon the Torah prohibition. Our Sages knew that a man would be put through excessive tests if not for the institution of these *harchakos*. They knew that the nature of a man is such that it would be nearly impossible for him to live with his wife in the same bedroom with no additional restraints.

Taharas hamishpachah is one of the principle vehicles which ensures that this *aizer k'negdo* relationship works. At times, a marriage requires this lesson of separation in order to give vitality to the physical aspect of the relationship. Our Sages are teaching us that the separation at the time of *niddah* helps to create a greater love. This separation is not required in any other relationship. Parents and children — and brothers and sisters — do not require a parting in order to enhance the relationship. This is a unique characteristic of marriage, and a key to its vibrancy. The observance of this mitzvah, therefore, carries with it a fringe benefit. It ensures that a marriage maintains its freshness and luster. Torah-observant Jews should never experience stagnation in marriage. Rather, with the progression of a marriage, there should be an ever-increasing bond.

This magnificent system is all the more pertinent for men, because without the *harchakos*, men would lack the self-control to avoid having relations. Yet these same *harchakos* need to be handled with great sensitivity, because this area can be quite difficult for one's wife.

For a woman, all these small gestures of expressing intimacy are most important. Because her emotions play such an important role, all of the seemingly little signs of intimacy are central to her at all times. But because the men need these stringencies, the women are deprived at this time of an important aspect of their intimacy. This is where the need for our great sensitivity comes into play.

Our Sages are not telling us to stop relating to our wives. They are not saying that we can't continue to have a wholesome and happy relationship with our wives. Sometimes, a man mistakenly thinks that because his wife is a *niddah*, he must show no signs of feeling towards her. Then, this same man, who has virtually ceased relating to his wife while she is a *niddah*, cannot understand why she is so cold toward him on the very night when she has come back from the *mikveh*. They haven't been together for almost two weeks, and he can't fathom why she is spurning his advances. He has just spent two weeks ignoring her and limiting his communication with her, reasoning that he mustn't show signs of intimacy. Now he is capable of simply changing gears from one type of relationship to another, while she doesn't respond to his overtures even when she is once again permitted to him.

A husband is capable of living with the *harchakos*

for two weeks, and at the end of these two weeks this pragmatic man, who has a lesser need for emotional input, can make the transition easily. He can be full of charm, while she is still simmering from what she perceives as being treated with rejection. So what can a man do to avoid this problem, which is rooted in the basically different personalities of man and woman?

The mitzvah of *onah* has broad connotations. It includes all of the emotional support which a husband is obligated to give to his wife. This mitzvah should not start in the bedroom on the night his wife comes home from the *mikveh*, nor should it start that morning. A man should be capable of differentiating between intimate expressions and expressions of care, concern and feeling and, therefore, the mitzvah should start two weeks before his wife's *mikveh* night. This aspect of the mitzvah of *onah*, the mitzvah in its broader sense, does not start and stop depending upon whether or not his wife is a *niddah*. The obligation to be close and a source of emotional support is a constant mitzvah. At all times, a woman should feel that she is the most important person in her husband's life.

The *halachos* which deal with marriage are not designed to be restraining and hampering. This should not be an area filled with tension or strife. It is an area which should bring added closeness to the relationship, and at no time is a man released of his obligation to give emotional support.

This should be a fulfilling, satisfying, pleasant and cementing area of marriage. If we don't rise up to this challenge of being sensitive to our wives when they are *niddos*, we are, in a sense, defeating the purpose spelled out by the Sages that the separation and reunion should become an enhancing factor in our marriages. If we approach this mitzvah with the right attitude, then it can, and will be, a major cementing element to help each one of us to build our own *mishkan me'at,* our own miniature sanctuary.

SIX

Creating an Atmosphere

There was once a traveler who, in the middle of a long journey, stopped at an inn. He was exhausted, and he needed to rest for a few hours before continuing his trip early the next morning. The innkeeper ruefully apologized and told him that there were no rooms available. The traveler pleaded. There must be one bed somewhere in the inn for just three or four hours.

The innkeeper had an idea. He told the traveler that there was a room which a general used, and if he promised to be out before 5 A.M., he could sleep in the general's bed. The grateful traveler assured him that he had to catch an early train, and that the general would never know that anyone else had slept in his bed. Everything was set.

Early the next morning, the innkeeper came flying into the general's room. "Quickly! Quickly!" he cried. "The general is coming. You must leave right away!" In a tremendous scramble, the traveler dressed and stuffed his belongings into his bag, barely eluding the general. There was only one problem. In his hurry, he accidentally put on the general's spare uniform.

Arriving at the train station, the traveler passed a mirror and saw himself in the general's clothes. Slightly confused, he exclaimed, "That foolish innkeeper! Instead of waking me, he woke the general!"

*   *   *

This parable, told by the Chofetz Chaim, teaches us a sharp lesson. A person can begin to behave in accordance with the status and images which have been imposed upon him by the outside world. He may have achieved levels of success in his career, but when he makes his journey back into the home, he must reassume the role of husband and father. Strutting around the house like a doctor, lawyer, teacher or businessman is not going to enhance his position in the family. He is not compromising his status at home if he sweeps the floor, changes a diaper or takes out the garbage. Difficult as it may be, we must be able to recognize our roles as husband and father as distinct from the proverbial clothes with which society adorns us.

Since it is usually the man who is out of the house, he is often in the role of coming home to his wife. It is crucial that we learn how to make the differentiation between home and work. Perhaps a man is a teacher. All day long, he is the biggest and smartest one in the classroom. Or perhaps he is a businessman. He has secretaries who listen to his every command. And now he's coming home. He must strip himself of the "general's clothes" and assume the role of husband and father. As a man comes into his home, he must make this transition.

As he enters his home and kisses the mezuzah, he should come back to the realization that he must shake off the outside world. This man is entering a new world; he is coming into the most important of his realities, his *mishkan me'at*. All of his tensions and problems must be left at the door when he kisses the mezuzah.

If a typical day for a man consists of a somewhat strenuous confrontation with his boss or colleagues, there is a piece of advice which can assist him in making this precarious transition from work to home. When he finds himself staggering home, focused exclusively on collapsing into his armchair and licking his wounds in peace, he may be rudely awakened to discover that other members of the family have also encountered their daily trials. They, too, are in great need of an ego massage. The husband who wishes to create a haven in his home for himself as well as for everyone else in the home will rally his last reserves of strength. Instead of coming in on a sour note, he will burst into the house with a smile and a good word for everyone. More often than not, this short introduction will set the tone for the evening and create a positive atmosphere in the home.

We must round up all of our energies to make this grand entrance. We have to realize that the first two minutes can set the tone for the rest of the night. If, after one has come into the home with a hearty greeting, told his wife how much he has missed her, swung the kids around and created a positive atmosphere — if after all of this, he still needs to collapse onto the couch, then, by all means, he should collapse.

The golden principle to remember is that moods are infectious. We cannot assume that our household will merrily continue on its way if we enter in a dark mood.

On the other hand, we assume with confidence that our positive, jovial countenance will soon affect the entire home.

SEVEN

The Key to Shalom Bayis

The Chazon Ish, in a letter directed to a husband in his first year of marriage, wrote the following:

"The nature of a woman is to derive pleasure from the amount of favor she finds in her husband's eyes, and she is constantly seeking to achieve this favor. Therefore, it is incumbent upon him to show her love and closeness through an abundance of conversation and expressions of fondness."

Men often want to know what the big "secret" is in *shalom bayis*. They expect a complicated formula to help them to make their wives happy. But, in the long run, it is the seeming trivialities which offer a big key to *shalom bayis*. Many men cannot fathom the power of a small gift, a quick phone call in the middle of the day, a well-placed compliment or any sensitive gesture. This concept is termed by our Sages as *ritzui* and *piyus*, appeasement and the creating of a congenial atmosphere (*Tur, Yoreh De'ah* 184). These are an integral part of a husband's obligation toward his wife. *Ritzui* and *piyus* form the framework for the mitzvah of *onah.* The Steipler Gaon (*Iggeres HaKodesh*) says that any type of endearing behavior by the husband which brings about a closeness is a fulfillment of the mitzvah of *onah.*

Many men are baffled by the potency of giving one's wife a flower. After all, reasons the pragmatic man, they cost money, they last but a short time and they are not even edible. But a small bouquet can move mountains. We should take care not to underestimate the power of the inexpensive gifts, the small notes, the sweet words and the short phone calls. No matter how busy the day is, there is time to pick up the phone to say a quick hello. If a man's wife is home, she has likely been cleaning, doing laundry and preparing dinner. On an average day, one household appliance has broken, one child has fallen and hurt himself, another child's teacher called to talk about a problem in the classroom. And now the phone is ringing. She thinks, "Now what!?!"

She picks up the phone to the "most sensitive husband in the world." He has called to say, "Hi, I'm thinking of you. I'm on my way home from work." He's taken out fifteen seconds to make this call, and he's made her day.

Every individual man needs to develop a sensitivity to his own wife and her particular needs. Is she moved by the occasional note? Does the phone call make her day? Is she touched because you picked up a small bouquet of carnations? This is one way to fulfill what the Steipler Rav (*Iggeres HaKodesh*) calls "the most essential hope of a woman . . . that she should be beloved to her husband." This is the *ritzui* and *piyus* of which our Sages spoke.

There is also an element of *ritzui devarim.* These are words which we know will be pleasing to our wives. The

Gemara teaches us the lesson of the great importance of these special words. Rav Kahana was a disciple of Rav. Being a diligent student, Rav Kahana wanted to know how Rav conducted himself in all of his personal matters. One night, Rav Kahana hid under Rav's bed to see how his teacher behaved when he was intimate with his wife.

Rav Kahana was astounded by what he discovered. Rav was a man about whom the Gemara testifies that he never spoke wasted words in his life. This was the man whom Rav Kahana knew. Yet when Rav was in the privacy of his bedroom with his wife, he chatted and laughed with her. He created an atmosphere of joviality (*Berachos* 62b).

We, too, need to laugh and create a congenial atmosphere with our wives. The Chazon Ish, in the above-mentioned letter, stresses that it is imperative for a man to relate to his wife in a friendly and light manner, using humor rather than seriousness and concern for his honor, as a way to create an atmosphere of closeness.

Most certainly, these gestures of buying gifts and making phone calls and behaving jovially have to be genuine. If we are being manipulative in order to have a doting wife, she will pick this up. Our Sages say, *"Devarim hayotzim min halev nichnasim el halev* — Words which come from the heart penetrate to the heart." Our intentions should be to fulfill the emotional aspect of the mitzvah of *onah* — to let your wife know that you think of her throughout the day. And gestures of this nature also have to be regular. One should not expect that one sweet act will magically create a continuously happy wife.

There is a story told of a couple having marriage problems. After a counselor spoke to both husband and wife, it came up that one of her concerns was that he didn't love her. When the counselor asked the husband if he loved his wife, he said, "Yes, of course." The counselor then asked him if he ever told his wife that he loved her. He said, "When we were married eighteen years ago, I told her I loved her. If things change, I'll let her know."

This is obviously far from the ideal. We need a little consistency and common sense. Our wives need constant appreciation, and the Torah obligates us to give it to them. The Chazon Ish also says in his letter that a woman's eyes are constantly lifted toward her husband in expectation of his appreciation.

Rav Yehuda Leib Chasman, the spiritual head of the Chevron Yeshivah in the 1920s, was giving a talk in the yeshivah when suddenly the village idiot ran in and gave a bang on the *bimah*, indicating that he had a very important announcement to make. With everyone's undivided attention, he proclaimed, "Gentlemen, I want to tell you that Reb Yehuda Leib Chasman is the greatest Jew alive. He's a *tzaddik* (pious man) and a *talmid chacham* (Torah scholar)." Before he could say more, they promptly tossed him out of the *beis medrash*, the study hall.

When Rabbi Chasman continued his talk, he told the students in the yeshivah, "I cannot tell you how much I enjoyed the address from that man. It was music to my ears."

We can learn from here an important lesson. Reb Yehuda Leib Chasman was a man of sterling character. He was far from being a person who suffered from low self-esteem. If such a man was pleased by personal compliments, even from the village idiot, how much more will our wives, constantly in need of appreciation, derive pleasure from our kind words. In truth, everyone enjoys hearing positive remarks about himself, and when said with sincerity and consistency, these positive statements can be an effective component in any relationship, certainly between husband and wife.

The wise man, knowing his wife's need for appreciation, is capable at all times of creating a healthy atmosphere by focusing on the positive, rather than looking to criticize and correct the negative. One can imagine a man coming home at the end of a hard day. He walks into his castle expecting to be treated regally. However, this particular day, his castle is practically upside down. Everything is a mess, and there's no hot dinner waiting for him. Now, assuming he is a perfect gentleman, he would never dream of yelling at his wife. Instead, exercising control, he says calmly, "It's a pity that supper isn't ready. It would be nice if you could have things ready when I get home." He has just lost the opportunity of creating a positive atmosphere, and, instead, he has succeeded in planting a hand grenade in the house.

If he's a man with sense, he'll look around. Something was sure to have survived the day. Perhaps a houseplant wasn't knocked over. He could then tell her how nice the plant looks. He could look for that one positive thing and praise it. As the author of the *Siddur Yaavitz* (Friday night prayers) phrases it, "It is a man's sacred obligation to feed his wife with words which gladden her heart."

We're looking for the big secrets to *shalom bayis*. We're looking for major issues. But it's these trivialities that will prove successful in creating *shalom bayis*. This is a major component in the role of the man. If a man finds that he's had a rough day and knows he won't be able to come home without his stresses from the day, he should stop for a snack or to wash his face. He must do whatever needs to be done, but come into the home smiling and create a positive atmosphere.

EIGHT

Quality Time

The Gemara in *Kesubos* (62b) teaches us that the frequency with which a husband is obligated to be with his wife in the actual intimate act is a function of his occupation. His occupation determines his availability to his wife. The Gemara speaks of several different levels of occupations, and, depending upon different aspects of his work, he may be obligated to be with his wife anywhere from once a day to once every six months. This same Gemara asks an interesting question. The Gemara queries, "What if a donkey driver wants to become a camel driver?"

The Gemara is talking about a case where the man was a donkey driver when he married his wife. The donkey driver makes his living by transporting people and goods on his donkey. The pay is very minimal, and his job can keep him away from home for a week at a time. Accordingly, the Torah obligates him to be with his wife once a week. Now he has the opportunity for a new job. He can become a camel driver. The camel driver is a far superior job as far as wages are concerned. His raise in pay will be ninefold. However, since the camel can travel for a much longer duration than the donkey, the camel driver has to be away from home for up to a month at a time. Correspondingly, the Torah obligates him to be with his wife only once every thirty days.

Rashi explains that when the Gemara asks, "What if a donkey driver wants to become a camel driver?" the question regards this man's wife. How will the wife of a donkey driver respond when her husband has the opportunity to become a camel driver? Does she prefer a more luxurious lifestyle, or does she prefer more frequent relations with her husband? The Gemara answers that a woman prefers a smaller income, though one that will ensure her of more frequent attention from her husband, to a ninefold increase in income, which brings with it a longer separation from her husband. The Gemara is teaching us about the nature of a woman. A woman is prepared to forgo life's material luxuries in exchange for her husband's attention.

A man might be misled into thinking that since he is young and in the process of building a career, his wife will understand if he can't give her the full attention that she needs right now. Perhaps she has even agreed to this. The Gemara is telling us about the essence of a woman. The most important thing in her life are the attentions that she receives from her husband, dwarfing even wealth and social status.

This attention is most crucial in the earliest stages of a marriage. The need for a man to attend to his wife's needs in the beginning of the marriage makes the challenge of building a successful marriage all the more formidable, because this is usually the time in a man's life when he puts in extra hours in order to build his career. The idea here is not to advocate that a man should ignore his responsibilities to earn a living. Rather, he should realize that it is very difficult to remedy a marriage which has been neglected in its earliest stages. A man needs to find the proper balance of quantity and quality. He must know that whatever time is allocated for home must not be spent recuperating from the day's work. He has to create true quality time.

Frequently, a man will make the claim that during the week it's impossible to spend time with the family, and on Shabbos he needs to recover from the week. And, of course, if there is extra time on Shabbos, there is so much learning and so many social obligations with which to catch up. Too often it happens that a lifetime slips by without one's having made quality time to bond with one's family. Shabbos must be a quality experience. The time spent with our wives and children must be quality time.

*   *   *

Rav Eliyahu Lopian, *ztz"l,* once told a story about himself when he was a young boy aged six or seven. His mother was in the habit of taking out all the dishes, glasses and cutlery once a month. She would put everything on the kitchen table so that she could clean the cabinets.

The boy was playing with his new ball when the inevitable happened. The ball landed on the table, and the dishes went flying. He was punished, and he learned his lesson. In the future, when it was time for his mother to clean, his plan was to keep far from the kitchen.

The next month, when cleaning day arrived, the young Eliyahu took extra special care that he would not cause his mother any trouble. But the Lopians had geese in the backyard, and sure enough, a goose came through the window and landed with a crash onto the dishes. Rav Lopian recalled that he said to himself, "Oh, is that goose gonna get it!"

He was amazed. His mother came along, picked up the goose, and dropped it back out the window. He remembered that he then said to himself, "I wish I were a goose." And he felt that way for a few weeks. Then one day his father came and slaughtered the goose, and it ended up on the Shabbos table. Reb Eliyahu recalled saying to himself that he no longer wanted to be a goose.

*   *   *

We need to learn to see our situation in a more mature light than a child sees his immediate situation. We must be able to see our own circumstances with a broader and lengthier view. We have to see how our time at home will effect our families in the long run, and we must make sure that our priorities are in order. If we are too quick to evaluate a situation and take action, we may lose sight of our ultimate, long-term objectives.

Achieving Holiness

We have presented some insights into the broader connotation of the mitzvah of *onah.* The specific aspect of this mitzvah is the ultimate physical act of intimacy. The Torah states, *"V'onasah lo yigra* — He shall not diminish her conjugal rights" (*Shemos* 21:10).

The fulfillment of this mitzvah, commanded only to the husband, is not an optional exercise. It is not a whim or a need, which one indulges. Rather, it is a positive commandment, clearly defined and controlled by halachah, Jewish law. The Steipler Gaon (*Iggeres HaKodesh*) defines it as a positive commandment, similar to the eating of matzah on Pesach night. He refers to a man who neglects to fulfill this mitzvah as an absolute sinner.

This mitzvah is completely independent from the mitzvah of *p'ru u'r'vu,* the command to be fruitful and multiply. It does not necessitate the potential of culminating in pregnancy. Rav Moshe Feinstein, *ztz"l,* wrote (*Iggeros Moshe, Even HaEzer,* 1:102), "The mitzvah of *onah* is not dependent on the possibility of conceiving. Rather, it is an obligation upon a man to see that his wife derives pleasure and that she should not endure sorrow or suffering. It is similar to his obligation to provide her with food and clothing... And therefore, he is obligated in the mitzvah of *onah* even if his wife is pregnant, post-menopausal or barren."

The Ramban (*Iggeres HaKodesh*) extols at length the benefits and merits of this mitzvah. He says, "When a man unites with his wife in holiness, the Shechinah, the Divine Presence, is found between them." Today, there is a prevalent negative perception of physical intimacies. Much of the non-Torah world refers to this negatively as pleasures of the flesh. Lest we should have such a perception, the Ramban states unequivocally, "One should know that marital union is holy and pure when it is done as it should be, at the time that it should be done and with the proper intent, and one should not think that there is anything disgusting or any ugliness, G-d forbid, in the proper union" (*Iggeres HaKodesh*, chap. 2).

The Vilna Gaon (*Shulchan Aruch, Even HaEzer* 557:53) succinctly explains how one can achieve these lofty levels of holiness through physical intimacy. He says that in order for one to achieve holiness at the time of relations, one should be *"yizaher miteisha hamiddos,"* one should be careful in regards to the nine categories which are discussed in the Talmud (*Nedarim* 20b). These *teisha middos* are categories of frames of mind which should not be present at the time of relations. If any of these *middos* are present when a couple is together intimately, it can be devastating to the relationship. Further, the damage which comes from such an act can have a negative effect on a child born from such a union. (These children can, however, choose to improve themselves since it is not predestined whether a person will be righteous or wicked [*Kehillos Yaakov, Yevamos*, 49].)

For our purposes, we will look briefly at these frames of mind to get a better insight into what links them together. Simple common sense dictates that these attitudes and situations are not ideal for relations, but what do they have in common that makes them so crucial that abstention from these *middos* is the key to holiness in marriage?

1. *B'nei s'nuah*, children of hate: The husband hates his wife. Relations are forbidden at this time, even if the hatred is kept secret from her (*Tur*).

2. *B'nei m'rivah*, children of quarrel: The Tur explains that this is an act of intimacy which comes in the middle of tensions and arguments. This applies even if there is no underlying hatred and the particular argument is an isolated incident.

3. *B'nei shichrus*, children of intoxication: Here Rashi tells us that because of his or her intoxication, this act is not complete, but it is an act of *z'nus*, prostitution. His or her only intention is for the physical act.

4. *B'nei grushas halev*, children of parents who have decided to divorce: This is an act of intimacy which takes place after a man has decided to divorce his wife. Even if they still love each other, yet some circumstance makes it impossible for them to stay together, this is a forbidden type of relationship.

5. *B'nei anusah*, children of coercion: These are relations against a woman's will. This includes physical force as well as verbal coercion (*Magen Avraham* 240).

6. *B'nei irbuviah*, children of mixture: Here, a man and his wife are intimate and the thoughts of either one are on someone else.

7. *B'nei nidui,* children of excommunication: There are relations when either one of the couple is in excommunication and is therefore not allowed to interact with anyone, including his or her spouse.

8. *B'nei t'murah,* children of exchange: Here, the man thought he was with another woman, and it turned out to be his wife.

9. *B'nei moredes,* children of a rebellious wife: There are relations with a woman who has declared that she will not fulfill her marital obligations.

The common link between all of these is that at the time of relations, either the husband and/or the wife is not focusing on enhancing or developing this relationship. A key component of *deveikus,* the intent to cement the relationship, is absent, and therefore the pleasures are totally nonproductive. When this is the case, the Torah forbids relations.

Using extreme care to avoid any of these *teisha middos* is what the Vilna Gaon says is the key to attaining holiness at the time of relations. When a husband and wife are certain that this intense act of intimacy is viewed as something constructive which will develop and enhance their relationship, then it is an act of holiness. This same act, which in many cultures is laden with guilt and regarded as spiritually detrimental, is seen as a principal vehicle for fulfilling the Torah commandment *v'davak b'ishto,* to cling to one's wife.

That cementing the relationship is the aim of physical relations is also seen from a comment of Rashi in the Gemara (*Niddah* 17a). The implication of the Gemara is that it is improper to have relations when one or both partners are asleep. Rashi explains that because of his being partially asleep, the man won't have a strong desire for his wife. His intention will be only to fulfill the mitzvah of *onah* or to please his wife, and Rashi says this is considered one of the *tisha middos*. We see that even if one has noble intentions, and, in fact physically satisfies his wife, yet due to his reluctance he lacks the specific goal of strengthening the relationship, this is not the proper manner of performing the mitzvah of *onah.*

Most people assume that the real reason that a man and woman have relations is simply because they have desires, and marriage is a legitimate outlet to indulge in these desires. However, we see that intimate relations are much more than a release of tension. Relations are a vehicle of holiness. G-d created within man and woman this tremendously intense desire in order that physical intimacy should be one of the principle vehicles for increasing love and oneness between them. This will ultimately introduce holiness into a couple's marriage.

In a similar vein, the *Sefer HaChinuch* says that the reason for the mitzvah of giving an extra level of attention to one's wife in the first year of marriage is *"k'dei l'hargil hateva imah u'lehadbik haratzon etzlah,"* in order to fuse their natures and desires. He's telling us that the purpose of this mitzvah is to help bring together these two people from entirely different worlds. When two people from totally different backgrounds and upbringings come together, there is a potential for great friction. The design of this mitzvah is to minimize this friction and help the couple unite on every possible level.

(Those interested in receiving more information on the topics discussed in this chapter, please see the attached coupon at the back of this book.)

True Love

One could look at the Torah's structuring of the mitzvah of *onah* and say that it is unfair. Why is the full burden placed only on the husband? How can this work if it's so one-sided?

This demand to look out exclusively for oneself is a malady of Western culture. We are constantly being told to be on the vigil lest someone dares to tread on our rights. Marriage is perceived as an arrangement whereby two individuals enjoy a total equality of rights and obligations. It seems, therefore, inconceivable that the major responsibilities of *shalom bayis* should not be equally shared.

Rav Chaim Shmuelevitz, *ztz"l,* offers an interesting insight into the source of the name of Moshe Rabbeinu, Moses, which also helps us to better understand this seeming lack of balance in the mitzvah of *onah.* We know that in the Hebrew language the name of something portrays its essence. A name has great significance, and a name of a person is definitive of his personality.

Our Sages tell us that Moshe Rabbeinu had ten

names. Each name described some aspect of his personality, and each name was representative of great spiritual capabilities. From all of these names, which is the one that Hashem selected for this man, the greatest of all Jewish leaders? Moshe.

The name Moshe was given to him by the daughter of Pharaoh because *"min hamayim m'shisihu* — from the water she drew him" (*Shemos* 2:10). But how could it be that the man who led the Jewish people out of Egypt was named after an action performed by a non-Jewish woman? Even though Moshe was completely passive, this is the name that was recorded for posterity.

Rav Chaim answers this puzzling question with an enlightening answer. This action of Pharaoh's daughter was one of extraordinary kindness and self-sacrifice. There was a decree from her wicked father to cast every Jewish child into the Nile, yet upon seeing this helpless child in the water, she risked her own life because of her great compassion and mercy.

Moshe Rabbeinu was the recipient of this kindness and self-sacrifice, and, as the recipient, these virtues became part and parcel of his personality. One who is on the receiving end of such great compassion and self-sacrifice naturally acquires these traits. It was the daughter of Pharaoh who instilled these virtues in Moshe. These qualities which Moshe needed to become the leader of the Jewish people were imbued in him by this non-Jewish woman. And because of her extraordinary generosity, Moshe takes on the name which recalls this act.

Rav Chaim says, in a similar vein, that parents who shower their helpless infant with love, care, and kindness will inject these virtues into their child. It is, perhaps, for this reason, that humans are born so totally helpless — in order that we may be the recipients of kindness and love. So too, by constantly pouring love and kindness into his wife, a husband fills her with these virtues. Her natural instinctive reaction will be, eventually, to respond in kind.

People often look at their spouses, see certain modes of behavior and character traits which they don't like and set out to change them. This is, at best of times, an almost impossible task and often a source of great conflict in the relationship. The most effective way of modifying someone's behavior is by showering upon the person acts of love and kindness. This will eventually elicit the desired response. In the framework of the mitzvah of *onah*, a husband is the one called upon to be the catalyst. By virtue of his inherent nature and pragmatism, this is his mitzvah, and it is incumbent upon him to be the initiator.

This whole idea of giving without necessarily receiving is really what love is. Love is, perhaps, the most distorted and misunderstood word in the English language. The root of the word "*ahavah*" (love) in Hebrew is "*hav*" (give). Love is created by giving. When we are compassionate, sensitive and responsive to our wives, it creates a love in ourselves, and this will eventually create a response from our wives toward us. This enables our two halves to become as one. (We also see that the numerical value of "*ahavah*" [love] is the same as the word "*echad*" [one].)

*   *   *

The story is told that Rav Yisrael Salanter, *ztz"l*, was once traveling on a train. In the same compartment with him was a young man who was behaving abusively toward this great man, not knowing that he was a leader of the Jewish people. Throughout the journey, he embarrassed

Reb Yisrael, treating him contemptuously as if the distinguished rabbi were some foolish old man. The train finally pulled into Vilna, and the whole town was waiting to meet this "old man," the great Reb Yisrael Salanter. The young man realized who he had been abusing and didn't know what to do.

The next morning, with tears streaming down his face, he came up to the rabbi's home to beg for forgiveness. Reb Yisrael forgave him and then proceeded to question him as to what he was doing in Vilna.

It turned out that this young man had come to Vilna to learn to be a *shochet* (a ritual slaughterer), but he had no plan for accomplishing his goal. Surprisingly, the rabbi took a great personal interest in this young man. He helped him find a place to live, a rebbe to teach him *shechitah* (ritual slaughter) and funds to help support him. Reb Yisrael Salanter went out of his way to treat him like a son.

At the end of the year, the young man came to Reb Yisrael and said that he understood that the rabbi had forgiven him, but he questioned Reb Yisrael as to why he had gone so far out of his way to treat him with such kindliness.

Reb Yisrael answered that his forgiving the young man was only lip service. In order to truly forgive him, Reb Yisrael knew that he had to take a special interest in the young man. In order to feel the love that the Torah demands ("*V'ahavta l'rei'acha kamocha* — And you shall love your friend as yourself"), he had to shower him with kindness and take this special interest in him. Now Reb Yisrael could say with confidence that he loved the young man and that he truly forgave him.

*   *   *

This is how we come to love our wives. By showering them with a multiplicity of kindnesses, we create love in ourselves, and we imbue our wives with this love. This ultimately becomes a two-way relationship. It is, however, the duty and challenge of the husband to begin this process. And hence, the obligation of the mitzvah of *onah* falls upon the husband.

This principle is illustrated by a parable attributed to the Maharam MiRottenberg. A person wanted to get an insight into the World to Come. He was taken to see Gan Eden and Gehinom (heaven and hell). First, he was taken to Gehinom. There he saw a magnificent banquet hall. Every possible delicacy adorned the tables. The elegance and grandeur was overwhelming. He saw this and thought, "This is Gehinom!?!"

But as he looked more closely, he saw that the "guests" were emaciated. They were starving to death. There was all of this exquisite food, but no one was eating. And why weren't they eating? Because strapped to each of their arms were three-foot-long knives and forks. Their arms were straight, and it was completely impossible for them to bend their elbows and bring the food to their mouths. Every pleasurable food in the world was there, but not a single one of them was partaking. A true Gehinom.

Next, he was taken to Gan Eden. Here he found the same exact setting with the same exact situation: a beautiful banquet hall, and here, too, the "guests" all had three-foot-long utensils strapped to their arms. But in Gan Eden, the people were all jolly and healthy looking. And in Gan Eden, they were eating. How was it that their situation was so much better than that of those in Gehinom? Upon closer study, he noticed that in Gan Eden, they were reaching across the table and feeding one another in such a way that they didn't have to bend their arms.

The person sitting in Gehinom is suffering there because that was how he approached life. He would walk into a situation, and he would always focus on himself. He was looking to fulfill his own needs. He would spend his entire life trying to bend his proverbial elbows and starve to death in the meantime. He was so focused on himself that he couldn't recognize others even to save himself from misery.

Then there is the person in Gan Eden. He is able to enjoy the pleasures that are there because of the way that he approached this world. In this world, he would walk into a situation, and the first thing he would notice was that the person across the table was hungry. Naturally, he would feed this man, and then this man would respond by noticing that he was also hungry. And they would feed each other.

A man is obligated to be completely focused on his wife's needs. He is the catalyst, due to his relative emotional stability. The objective of this mitzvah is to give pleasure to one's wife. There is nothing said about the man's needs. There is no reciprocal mitzvah. Hashem created the world in such a way that through a man's satisfying his wife's needs, he becomes satisfied. This is man's nature. By focusing on her needs, he will inevitably receive pleasure. There is an art to fulfilling this mitzvah, and it is to focus on one's wife's needs.

This is true for nearly every facet of the couple's relationship. His personal needs are relegated to secondary importance. He needs to focus on his wife's needs. On the physical level, his nature is such that by endeavoring to satisfy his wife's needs, his own needs are fulfilled. The Ramban (*Iggeres HaKodesh*) states that the pursuit of pleasure for one's self will ultimately result in discord. Not only does he not fulfill the mitzvah, but he, instead, creates a negative situation.

*　　　*　　　*

The Midrash tells a story of two brothers. These brothers each had a plot of land on either side of a mountain. One brother had a large family, while the other had no children.

The brother with no children thought to himself, "My poor brother. He must be so sad with no children to gladden his heart. The least I can do for him is to give him a sheaf of wheat from my crop." Not wanting his brother to detect him, he took a bundle of wheat, crossed the mountain which was between their homes and stealthily put the wheat in his brother's storehouse.

Meanwhile, on the other side of the hill, the brother with no children was also thinking. He said to himself, "My brother and I have the same size plot of land, and yet he has so many more mouths to feed. It must be very difficult for him. I know what I'll do. I'll sneak across the mountain and put a bundle of my wheat into his storehouse."

And so for a long time these two brothers would pass each other in the thick of night, going to deliver a bundle of wheat. Each one noticed in amazement in the morning that his own supply was not diminishing.

Finally, one night, as each brother was climbing the mountain with his sheaf of wheat, their paths crossed. They looked at each other, and each one suddenly understood why his supply had not been diminishing. The two brothers embraced, and both cried from their deep love of each other. Hashem saw this and decided that this would be the spot where the Holy Temple would be built.

*   *   *

Marriage is likened to a *mishkan me'at,* a microcosmic version of the Holy Temple. In order to create a sanctuary of love, peace and harmony, where G-d will enter and dwell, it is imperative that *ahavah* (love) permeates the relationship. This must be an *ahavah* whose root is *hav* (giving).

Men and women seeking guidance on being true Jewish husbands and wives in any country may obtain further information from the International Office of Jewish Marriage Education:

POB 18103
Jerusalem 91180

or may contact —

JME
29 Park Ave.
Monsey, N.Y. 10952
tel: 914-426-6678
fax: 914-426-2268

or

JME
64 Whitehall Road,
Gateshead,
NE8 4ET,
England
tel/fax: 091-477-0620